The Queen's Queue

Laura O'Boyle

Copyright© 2023 Laura O'Boyle
All rights reserved.
ISBN: 9798391240570

This book is for my daughters Amy and Emily. Thank you for being my inspiration in everything that I do.

Acknowledgements

With grateful thanks to my Dad who edited each chapter as I wrote. Also to my Mum for editing my Dad's editing. Thank you to Paul, Amy and Emily for giving me the time to indulge in writing. Thank you to my Uncle Danny for allowing me to include his poem. Lastly, thank you to Janet for her good company in the queue.

CONTENTS

Chapter 1	Rest in Peace Your Majesty	Page 6
Chapter 2	What3words	Page 21
Chapter 3	The Southwark Snake	Page 37
Chapter 4	The Great British Queue	Page 53
Chapter 5	Wristbands	Page 69
Chapter 6	Bridge Houses	Page 83
Chapter 7	Mud and Memories	Page 97
Chapter 8	Old London Town	Page 110
Chapter 9	Bankside	Page 123
Chapter 10	Her Majesty Queen Elizabeth II	Page 138
Chapter 11	This is St. Bartholomew's Fair	Page 151
Chapter 12	The Queen's Walk	Page 166
Chapter 13	Bag drop	Page 182
Chapter 14	Hearts for Covid	Page 195
Chapter 15	The Westminster Snake	Page 209
Chapter 16	Westminster Hall	Page 223

Chapter 1
Rest in Peace Your Majesty

Everyone remembers where they were when the Queen died. It is one of those events in history that shocks, saddens and ultimately leads to hours of avid TV and news watching. Everything gets pushed to the 'to do' list whilst we camp out in front of the screen, awaiting the snippets of information that will feed our curiosity and provide cliff-hangers to even further news stories for the next day.

Social media becomes a place fuelled with opinions, stories and declarations of solidarity grief. 'Rest In Peace Your Majesty', 'The Queen has died', 'Thank you for your dedication and service', messages flash up on all channels. Images of the Queen as a baby, child, mother, grandmother and serving monarch fill our screens. Poems, anecdotes, memoirs, Biblical verses and more capture the nation's mood. Everybody wants to pay their respects and the first port of call for doing so is online.

It all started on a Thursday afternoon with the headlines 'Members of the Royal Family make their way to Balmoral to be at the Queen's bedside.' What did this mean? Is she unwell? Which members of the Royal Family were attending? Wasn't she only just photographed with the new prime minister Liz Truss this week? As I saw the news notification appear on my mobile, I couldn't help but tell those around me. The need to discuss, debate and process was pretty intense for all. "The Queen is dying, the family have gone to her", I heard myself saying aloud.

My audience was a secondary school class all 'apparently' working hard in their lesson. The questions started, 'How do you know?' 'Was she unwell?' Is she going to die?' Then the stories started,

"Miss I saw the Queen once..."

"Miss I've been to Buckingham Palace... "

I read aloud to the students, "Following further evaluation this morning, the Queen's doctors are concerned for Her Majesty's health and have recommended she remain under medical supervision." The class erupted into discussion. I then erupted into a bit of a panic. When would I learn not to think aloud in class, I wondered to myself.

I was the key disrupter here, not Johnny in the corner throwing mini snowballs of paper around the room. Then again, was it ok on this occasion to share this news? After all this was the Queen about which we were talking. She was obviously in her last moments and it was breaking news. Surely this is ok to share with the class and discuss our thoughts and feelings? It might be difficult to get back onto the curriculum path this lesson but education is not just about getting through the power point, its current affairs, it's showing ourselves, as teachers, as human. We are in England and the Queen is obviously in her last moments. This was important to share. I had done the right thing.

Negative thoughts of questioning myself aside, I knew that most students in the class were interested and would be going home to families doing exactly what I was planning to do. Putting on the news and settling down with a cup of tea.

I began to recollect other events from years before. They would set the scene for my days ahead, namely one in particular, the death of the Princess of Wales in 1997. I remember where I was when Princess Diana died. Who doesn't? I was only eighteen at the time, not what I would call a true monarchist but British and proud nevertheless.

My Saturday night had consisted of a small gathering at my cousin's house as her parents were away. You can imagine what state we all got into. A bunch of 18-year-olds, no parents. I remember running out of cigarettes and ordering a minicab to go to the shop for us and buy some more. I guess it was the Deliveroo or Uber of the 1990's. Cab drivers were there to shop for us if we needed and we needed to smoke.

Following an evening that I can't even pretend to remember, I was awoken early to one hungover friend telling us all to get up, wake up, Princess Diana had died. He spoke with urgency and we all rushed to the front room to turn on the television. Pink flowery sofas with wheels on a parquet floor. Such fun to move around and get closer to the TV. We kept the green velvet curtains closed. I'm not sure why? Maybe **defiance**. We were not greeting this new day. Our heads didn't want to, our bodies didn't want to and we were teenagers after all. It's a given that we shouldn't open curtains until the evening.

We camped out in front of the TV watching the news with disbelief all day continuing the smoking and drinking from the night before. The images in front of us were unbelievable. We sat in mostly companiable silence drinking it all in, in more ways than one.

Come Monday morning, inevitably, none of us were fit enough for work and I had to phone in sick. I regaled my unwellness on the phone whilst my cousin Martine hid on the floor the other side of the bed giggling. This was a time before mobile phones. A time when homes had an 'upstairs' and 'downstairs' landline. I had gone upstairs for privacy, but it wasn't to be and I soon ended up giggling myself as I lied about a dodgy curry and my nether end situation. I wonder if my boss realised and heard the giggles. The guilt was too much. In fact, to this day, I've not had a sick day without actually being sick. I felt so bad for lying and vowed never to be sick from work again unless I really was unwell.

As we recovered from our hangovers, the week brought with it more news and news full of flowers. Such amazing flowers and displays of grief. I had to join. I felt compelled to join, not because I'm a hardened royalist but because I'm British. That's what we do. British people mourn together, celebrate together and respect our monarchy and those associated with it, together. I could see the sadness, the overwhelming deep respect shown by the public on the news. I wanted to join. Princess Diana was 'the' celebrity of that era. We were living through history. On reflection, isn't everyone, everyday, living through history? I decided to go at the end of the week (no more sick days for me) and witness for myself the scenes on the TV.

The sea of flowers that greeted me as I arrived at Kensington palace a few days later was unreal. The smell. I can still smell that flowery sweet smell and see the tears falling from faces all around me. I couldn't quite believe the depth of the flowers. Totally wowed by the outpouring of love for someone that most people had never met. Moved, ever more shocked, I retreated to the back of the crowds to sit and take it all in, estimating the depth of flowers. They were up to my knees, deeper in places. I wanted everyone to see what I could see. I closed my eyes and tried to capture the image in my memory forever. It worked, I have yet to forget.

The news watching then continued until the funeral when we would all feel distraught on behalf of William and Harry. The images of them walking behind their mother's coffin have become iconic for all the wrong reasons. Should they have had to do that? The debate is still open.

Diana's brother was in the news. More detail and information to retain and hold onto. Seeing him alongside the coffin led to more realisation that this was simply a woman, a daughter, a mum and a sister. The public still could not get enough of Diana. Sad and ironic that this was also the same before her death and in many eyes, a reason for her death. I remember watching the funeral and thinking one day I will visit her grave. 25 years later and that day is still yet to come.

My first memories of a major royal event. Not a celebration. Not a happy occasion, but sadness and tragedy and public mourning in a way unseen before.

Fast forward 14 years and it is time to celebrate in true British fashion the wedding of William and Kate! Armed with newspapers, cakes and my five year old daughter decked out in a bridesmaid dress to celebrate, I arrived at my sisters to join the family party and celebrations. My mum turned up with her wedding veil and my daughter and nieces proudly paraded around the front garden holding the end of it, all dressed up in their special dresses. Not only was it a special day for William and Kate but a special day for us as we celebrated as a family and indeed for the whole of Britain as we imagine and consider the impact this couple would have on our lives in the years to come. We all cheered when they kissed on the balcony and left our party happy, satisfied and ready for more. Full up with sausage rolls, sandwiches, cakes and tea. The food items have now become a tradition of mine for royal occasions.

Seven years later and the sausage rolls are once again in the oven, the sandwiches prepared, cakes made and teapot ready. This time it's Harry and Meghan's turn. Excited that my youngest daughter was now joining in the fun, we all had a day in front of the TV with our picnic watching with delight as Meghan arrived, followed by the ceremony which happened to include one of my favourite all time hymns, 'This little light of mine'. I used to play it often when I worked at a special needs school and the students used to love it, clapping their hands and stamping their feet. Such a joyful tune.

We all had a great day at the wedding in the front room. Amy was now aged 12 and Emily aged 6. I was glad to share the experience with them both. In true Paul style my husband claimed to be uninterested but of course sat through a great deal of the news coverage, enjoying it as much as us I'm sure. He does the same with the reality programmes I watch. Always complaining that they aren't any good yet silently watching alongside me.

Smaller occasions of news watching with a cup of tea include all the royal births of course. This is a family that represents us all, looks out for us all and works hard to raise awareness of various causes. The least we can do is show our respect.

Respect. Now there's a word. It is a word I heard many times in the queue for the Queen. "We thought we would come to pay our respects".

The 6th February 2022 marked a marvellous period in history. The Queen became the first British Monarch to celebrate a Platinum Jubilee, marking 70 years of service to the people of the United Kingdom, the Realms and the Commonwealth. To celebrate this wonderful service to the people, a four day bank holiday weekend was announced! Was I excited to celebrate the Queen or excited about the prospect of more sausage rolls, tea and cake? Both! I began to purchase Union Jack plates, cups and a royal bingo game for a weekend of fun and celebration. We decided to spend the weekend at a holiday park in Norfolk. Bunting was coloured in, cakes made with mini flags and the picnic was packed. We were ready to celebrate. A large party on the green was planned. Decked out with our camping chairs, picnic blanket and picnic we made our way to join the celebrations. A bar provided some cool drinks on a warm summer's day. Paul and Emily decided to go for a swim in the pool next to the party. Amy and I got a drink and relaxed into the atmosphere (and the chairs) with our dog Buddy. A singer provided the entertainment with some old classics. I knew some of them but not all. Nevertheless, plenty of people around me knew them and joined in the singing. Happy and joyful. This is what the monarchy does. It brings people together to celebrate. I was loving every minute of it. It reminded me of films I had seen with people at parties, dancing, singing and celebrating the end of the war. Flag flying patriotism. Who doesn't love a good knees up?

The weekend brought with it some fabulous TV watching with more cups of tea and cake and heartfelt warm feeling towards the Queen and her service to this country. I can't begin to tell you that I know the full extent of her work and service because I don't. However, I do have a deep respect for her and her commitment and passion towards the people of Britain and the Commonwealth.

Buses representing each decade travelled down Birdcage Walk with celebrities from different eras waving and cheering. What fun! I couldn't name them all but there were certainly some familiar faces. My husband being six years older knew a few more than me! Then there were the interviews with those that have served the Queen. Her former piper. Wow, she had a piper play her music each morning. What a wonderful way to wake up. Having lived in Scotland for two years, aged 23-25, I have a love for Scottish music. A personal piper does seem somewhat of an indulgence. However, if I was The Queen working until my final week on earth I would want a piper playing to me daily as well. She deserved it.

Then there was the concert! Prince Louis making his cousins laugh and Prince George and Princess Charlotte enjoying the fun and clearly on their best behaviour. Everyone loves a glimpse of the royal children. Twice I have visited Osborne House on the Isle of Wight and it's the royal children's quarters that always capture my attention and imagination. The cots, beds and dolls houses. Queen Victoria's children even had their own cabin to learn and store their collections from nature. How lucky they were! Yet from historical accounts perhaps not so lucky with a mother reluctant to show emotion and affection towards them or so the story goes.

Back to the Platinum Jubilee celebrations. What a happy, fun celebratory weekend. The fly past spelling out 70 and the Royal Family on the balcony. The light show above Buckingham Palace. Images to warm the heart including, of course, the much loved teapot. It had certainly become a big part of my royal celebrations over the years. The pre-recorded clip of the Queen having tea and sandwiches with Paddington has become well known the world over. The Queen always has a bag with her and now we know what she keeps inside it. Marmalade sandwiches.

The Queen wasn't well enough to make the concert in person. Aged 96 it was understood and expected. I had started to worry in the lead up to the celebrations that the Queen might not make it at all and it would all be cancelled. Thankfully she lived and has gone down in history as the longest serving monarch.

Back to September 2022 and the class full of secondary school children. We managed to get through our lesson without any further disruption from me, but our thoughts were with the Queen. If the family were travelling to be with her and this news had leaked, there must be a reason.

At 3pm, I ushered everyone out quickly and headed to the office to tell everyone the Queen might be dying. Aged 96 this should not be unexpected. But somehow it seemed to be. Over the next few days and weeks, many people spoke of the unexpected loss they felt. The shock at feeling so much over someone they had possibly never met. The thing was, the Queen had been there throughout all our lives. A constant force, representation and inspiration.

My mind turned to my Grandma who had died in November 2021 aged 96 herself. What would she make of all this I wondered. I would think about my Grandma a lot over the coming days. Her life and her death.

Once home, in front of the TV and with my mobile next to me to scroll the news, I awaited. Messages flashed up, one from my sister Sarah. "BBC news reporters are wearing black ties, this doesn't look good." We awaited the announcement. We didn't have to wait long.

"A few moments ago, Buckingham Palace announced the death of Her Majesty Queen Elizabeth II. The Palace has just issued this statement. It says, "The Queen has died peacefully at Balmoral this afternoon. The King and the Queen Consort will remain at Balmoral this evening and will return to London tomorrow." This was repeated over and over. Oh my goodness the Queen has actually died. The Queen. No longer. Why was I shocked? What were these feelings I hadn't expected?

The news brought statements from King Charles III. King Charles! We have a King! "The death of my beloved mother, Her Majesty the Queen, is a moment of the greatest sadness for me and all members of my family. We mourn profoundly the passing of a cherished sovereign and a much-loved mother. During this period of mourning and change, my family and I will be comforted and sustained by our knowledge of the respect and deep affection in which the Queen was so widely held."

The prime minister came out of Downing Street to speak. As I watched I wondered how long this speech had been prepared. At the end 'God save the King' was spoken for the first time. I felt shivers down my spine. This was truly major news.

News of 'Operation London Bridge is down' filtered through the internet. Wait a minute. I'd heard of Operation London Bridge. This was the code name for when the Queen died. What was this surreal world I was living in? I was beginning to feel like I was living through historic moment after historic moment. The covid years, the lockdowns, the home schooling, war in Europe and now the Queen has died. There was only one thing for it.

Make a pot of tea.

Chapter 2
what3words

I knew when I had changed jobs three years earlier that it was the right thing for myself and my family to work four days a week. It allowed me to be a better mum and a better teacher. I could be there for my children on my day off, Fridays, taking to school, collecting from school, arranging playdates. All the 'messages' as they say in Scotland, could be done on my day off, from collecting prescriptions to shopping to spending more time with the newest addition mentioned earlier, Buddy the cavapoo.

Not to mention the occasional meeting of friends for coffee, the hour watching 'Homes under the Hammer' or the very occasional afternoon snooze to recharge. (I have to say 'very occasional' as my husband may be reading this and I don't want him to think this is why I relish my days off.)

As the Queen had died on a Thursday, it meant I had a full three days of catching up with the news. I could spend my Friday understanding what had happened and what was going to happen in the coming weeks. I decided I would once again camp out in front of the TV for the day drinking tea.

Everyone was awaiting the funeral date announcement which would take some time. Of course, there was lots of talk as to whether a day off work would be announced. Not only lots of talk, but lots of hope. Not just to avoid work but so that focus could be given to the funeral. If it took place at the weekend, people were busy and had plans. If it was on a day that was supposed to be work, no plans had been made. Therefore, more attention on the funeral and time to pay final respects. Of course, there were the teenagers at school who purely wished for a week day funeral so that they could have the day off school.

We soon learnt that Princess Anne had been with the Queen in her last moments. Once again my thoughts turned to my Grandma. She had died aged 96. Also as it happens, on a Thursday. She didn't have Princess Anne with her when she died but she did have me. Her granddaughter. It was me that was with her in the last moments of life.

She had spent the last three years of her life in a care home. A wonderful care home that looked after her in a way we could only have hoped for. She joined in with various activities and made friends. From singers, to cooking, to puzzles to having her nails done. I saw my Grandma smile more in the care home than I had probably seen in my entire life.

My family had known a couple of weeks before her death that she was in her last moments. My parents, aunts, uncles and cousins all visited to spend time with her in her last weeks. As with many deaths, time seems to go slow when you are waiting for someone to die. You begin to think every breath is the last but it never seems to be.

On November 4th 2021, having visited a couple of times over the week, I left work in my blue spotty dress that my colleague said reminded her of Miss Honey from Matilda and I made my way to the care home. Stocking up with Red Hot Monster Munch and a Kit Kat Chunky from a petrol station, I ate it quickly thinking that I must need food to keep me going in case I am late home for dinner.

As I arrived my aunt and uncle were just leaving. I waited outside Grandma's room for them to say goodbye. My mum and dad had also just arrived so we sat together with Grandma playing some hymns. She was a Catholic. She also classed herself as French. A few days earlier she had lifted her hands to orchestrate as she heard the French national anthem being played. Her mother was from Belgium, her father from France.

The reason she was playing out the end of her life in a care home in Essex was because she had met an English soldier in the Second World War and came to England as his bride. The rest they say is history. I had always thought my Grandma identified as Belgian but French it was.

My cousin Jane popped in whilst I was there. It was her birthday. She had spent a lot of time with Grandma in her final days, even acting as priest and reading a full mass to her with a little holy water sprinkled instead of communion. Bless you Jane.

After an hour or so it was time for my parents to leave. I decided to hang on a little longer. I held her hand. My Grandma. Marie Yvonne Duvin. I played some music on my phone. Mama by Il Divo followed by Gregorian chant music. I began to say the rosary out loud. Within an hour she had died.

I knew it was her last moments in the last 10-15 minutes. I could tell by her breathing. Something had changed. I couldn't phone my Dad as it would disturb the very peaceful music playing. I had a fleeting thought to consider my options. If I turned off the music on my phone to make the call, her last sense of hearing would be me telling Dad to hurry quick. There just didn't seem to be a chance between the praying and speaking to her and music. No-one would have got there on time. It was her very last breaths. My focus intensified as I leant in, squeezed her hand tight and continued to talk and pray.

So, there I was saying the Hail Mary with Gregorian chant in the background. I told her we loved her and I knew she would look forward to seeing my Grandad and Uncle Paul. She had spent her life a bereaved woman having lost my Grandad Jack when he was 59 and losing her grown up son Paul aged 38. She had never fully recovered from these losses.

I told her we knew she loved us too and that I was there as the whole family and that we were all there holding her hand and she would be ok. As she passed, I continued to pray and hold her hand. I waited approximately five minutes then went to get help.

"My Grandma isn't breathing".

"They do that sometimes, let's have a look".

Two care workers followed me into Grandma's room. One of them held her wrist and within a couple of seconds turned to me and said "You're right, she's definitely gone".

Hugs all round. I almost felt like an intruder as I wasn't the most frequent visitor to Grandma. I also felt privileged and so grateful that I was able to be with her on behalf of all the family. Out of everyone it was me that she died with. It was a special moment between us. A moment shared. Just me and Grandma. Only deep down I knew it wasn't just me with her. I was her whole family in those moments, representing us all.

As I stood in the queue for the Queen nearly a year later, holding my Red Hot Monster Munch, my go to food to sustain me in times of emotion, I was again representing all those that couldn't be there. Kay from the office, Sarah with her bad back and parents too old to stand for long.

The spiritual feeling of one representing all was with me once more. Not only was I representing those in the present that couldn't be there, but those from the past also. All those that had been part of the Queen's reign. We were representing them all.

My Friday the day after the Queen died began like any other, yet was unlike any other. With the school run over, I spent most of the day on the sofa surfing the web and watching the news. 'God save the King!' was repeated regularly and I felt as though I was living in some sort of history movie. I hadn't realised there would be such tradition surrounding the Queen's death. I was drawn to it, sucked in, wanting to know more.

We all awaited the funeral date which was announced for Monday 19th September. A day off work for many! An even longer weekend for me with my Friday's off. I would really be able to drown in all the pageantry. Sausage rolls were added to my online shopping. This time I was going to make my own cakes and shortbread and enjoy a tea party whilst paying respects to the Queen.

Considering I wouldn't call myself a royalist, the scrap book had been bought and I had begun to collect newspapers for my youngest daughter, Emily. She worked on it with my mum and decided to create a page for each of the Queen's decades that she lived. A lovely idea I thought.

Before I knew it, the weekend was over and we were back in the routine of work and school again. The news watching and internet scrolling had to stop. My mind turned to life beyond the screen and social media tributes. I felt compelled to pay my respects in person. Despite some anxiety at using the London Underground, I found myself on the tube on the way to see the flowers with my eldest daughter Amy on the Monday after school.

As we arrived the crowds were phenomenal, yet controlled and respectful. Queues edging forwards towards Buckingham Palace, slow moving but nevertheless moving, greeted us as we came out of a side road onto Birdcage Walk. Joining the moving queue, which can only be described like an ant hill, all scurrying, edging their way to the top of the hill. In our case, Buckingham Palace.

We admired the flowers, taking the usual tourist photo outside the gates before twisting round towards Green Park where the flowers were. Again, the queue always moving, full of humans with the same cause.

Upon entering the park we were met with such beautiful displays of love and grief. Paddington Bear seemed to take a lead role. He has become something of an icon since sharing that marmalade sandwich clip with the Queen for her Platinum Jubilee.

Amy was wowed by the flowers. I was perhaps less so. The organisation was clear for all to see. It felt different from the impromptu flower laying for Princess Diana.

We were able to walk around the Queen's flowers on paths that had been created and such precision and consideration had led to a feeling of safety and comfort. It felt more like a display than an outpouring of grief. It was organised and felt special to be part of. Anyone who was anyone seemed to be there. The elderly, young, children, locals, tourists. Everyone was welcome with their common aim being a moment to remember the Queen.

Having spent some time reading heartfelt condolences we moved on. Once again into a moving queue. We were hustled along, especially the area where we crossed Birdcage Walk. So many people were stopping to take photos and stewards were shouting out to keep moving and not to stop as the cameras flashed. Again, safety was evidently high priority. Thank goodness as I wouldn't say I was very good with crowds. If you have ever left Wembley Stadium at the end of a concert or a football match you will know how daunting crowds can be. This was different. It wasn't a frenzy. Whoever had the task of public order following the Queen's death had done a great job.

As the news shifted throughout the week from Queen to King to Princes and Princesses something was beginning to feature slowly and then more prominently. The queue for the Queen lying in state.

The Queen's Queue.

As if the Paddington Bears, the ceremonial declarations and the endless cups of tea weren't enough. We now had a true British tradition forming in front of our eyes. A queue to end all queues. Not only was this queue the most organised queue we had ever seen but it also became the most watched queue ever seen. We were no longer watching news on the Queen but watching news of the people queueing for the queen. We were watching a queue... and loving it. The queue had its own website explaining to wannabe queuers where to go to find the end of the queue at any given time. I found myself explaining to my friends on whatsapp what 'what3words' meant as everyone was engrossed in the detail of the queue.

What3words was created in 2013 in London. It identifies precise locations of about 3 metres by using three words. For example navy.noises.overnight points to a location in Southwark Park. This enabled queuers to pinpoint the end of the queue by a precise location so that they could make their way to join the queue.

The live queue tracker had a map of the queue, the approximate mileage, estimated queueing time, nearest landmark and what3words. The people of Britain began not only watching the people in the queue but also watching the end of the queue move via what3words. Modern technology at its best.

The live video tracker was created by the Department for Digital, Culture, Media and Sport and had almost 10 million views. Even those not joining the queue were watching the queue tracker.

"These people must be mad queueing for hours" some people said. Yet what seemed madder was the people watching the people queue. Drones filmed thousands snaking their way along the Southbank. At first the queue was four hours long with the end of the queue near the

Millennium Wheel. Then it was six hours then eight then nine then ten. It was growing and growing.

Tentatively I voiced to my sister Sarah than I might like to go and pay my respects to the Queen lying in state.

"Thursday evening might be good" I said, "as then I have Friday off to recover". These Fridays were becoming very handy it seemed. It turned out that this didn't suit my sister and I certainly didn't fancy queueing overnight with strangers in the dark and cold. Or did I?

One week since the Queen had died and it was Thursday again. I found myself standing in Tesco's considering what food I might like to take to walk the queue. I had finished work for the weekend and I felt compelled to pay my respects. This was it. I was going to go it alone! Friday morning, I was going to queue to see the Queen. Decision made. No going back. I had come to the realisation that queueing alone was actually my preferred method. A mini holiday. Time out. No-one to worry about except myself.

As I browsed the meal deals, I found myself looking at a coronation chicken sandwich. How apt! Coronation for the Queen. Perfect. Okay this wasn't her coronation but it was still a royal word so I'll make it fit. Some Red Hot Monster Munch will go nicely with that. Hot cross buns too because who doesn't have hot cross buns when they are going on a journey? A Snickers might be nice for some energy. Some Starburst for my pocket. Perfect.

As I walked through the door announcing that I was going to see the Queen lying in state, Paul, Amy and Emily laughed and thought I must be mad.

"When are you going?" said Paul.

"Tomorrow. It's my day off remember. Perfect timing. If I take Buddy for his groom at 10:30 then get the train, you can collect the dog and get the girls from school."

"You don't even like public transport, how are you going to do this?" Paul exclaimed. I hadn't really thought that bit through but I was determined. I was going to do this. I wanted to do this. Nothing was in my way. I had the day off work. I had Paul available to collect the girls from school. The weather looked dry. Indeed, I was really looking forward to the 8-10 hour alone time. Life is busier than it has ever been for so many of us. I couldn't wait to have some peace and quiet.

"I'll manage" I replied, then headed upstairs with a smile, to download some Bee Gees and Chris De Burgh onto my phone.

Right, next bit of my attention, the bag. Not too big, not too small. I had the perfect mini rucksack. Thank goodness because the bag drop in the queue was not in the queue at all but a ten minute walk out of the queue I found out the next evening. So, what shall I take? Food of course. My beloved picnic. That can all go in a plastic bag as it will be eaten by the time I get to the front of the queue. No point taking up precious room in my bag for consumables.

Purse, umbrella, woolly hat, iPad with The Crown downloaded to watch, phone with some good playlists ready, earphones, paracetamol, asthma pump, tissues. What else did I need? Scarf, gloves... the list went on. I soon realised the bag wasn't big enough. Time for some decluttering.

Right, paracetamol doesn't need the box. I know what they are. Gloves can fit in coat pocket. Purse? I'll just take some cash and bank card. This was better. Now there was room for everything that I needed. Oh and my new biography book for children. Queen Elizabeth II by Sally Morgan. Now I was ready. I couldn't wait. Not only was I going to see the Queen lying in state but I was going to have hours by myself with Netflix, a book and a good soundtrack. What middle aged working mum wouldn't want this opportunity? What an adventure I was going to have. I felt empowered. Brave even.

As word spread that I was heading to the queue I would even go so far as to say slightly popular too. Ping ping ping went my Whatsapp messages.

'Heard you were queueing, hope not too cold!'

'If I had known you were queueing I'd have taken the day off to join you'.

'How are you getting home? It might be the middle of the night by the time you come out?' Good old mum. Always there to worry about me. 'We'll pay for a taxi home'. That was the best message of all. No need to worry about afterwards. Straight into a taxi for me and home to bed. Right, I'm all set. Let's do this!

Friday morning arrives. Ok so my usual Skechers without socks might not hit it in the coldness of the evening, so I go for socks and trainers. Jeggings, t shirt and jumper. Layers, always layers if you aren't sure.

My jumper had white visible writing on a navy background. Ideal for Paul to spot me on the TV. Then my coat. Perfect. I'm ready.

Just then the phone rings. It's my mother-in-law.

"Hi Sue", I say bright and cheery.

"Hi Laura, I hear you're off to see the Queen. My cousin really wants to go but doesn't want to go alone, so I've given her your number so you can meet and keep each other company".

"That's great!" I say as I look over at my bag with all my solitary entertainment excitement disappearing by the second.

Chapter 3
The Southwark Snake

"Hi Janet, it's Laura here, Sue's daughter in law".

"Hello, oh I'm so pleased to hear from you. So we are doing this? Where shall we meet?" came the voice down the phone. The gratitude and excitement melted away any concerns I had about missing out on my Netflix and Chris De Burgh. I was happy to help. This was about community. Not selfish desires to abandon my family and have 10ish hours to myself.

"I'm so pleased Sue gave me your number. I've been wanting to queue but just couldn't do it alone".

"It will be lovely to queue with someone" I heard myself replying. "Let's meet at Canada Water" I proposed, having carefully planned my route from Chingford. Anyone that has a bit of public transport anxiety will know that planning is important.

"I don't think I can get there, can we meet at London Bridge then go together?"

"Of course we can!" I replied, quickly searching **TFL** map and rerouting my journey.

"Great! I'll be wearing a pink coat. Where shall we meet?"

"If you head out of London Bridge station, towards the bus station, there's a card shop. Let's meet there." Suddenly, I was the London expert, the transport expert. Yet anyone that knows me will know that this is far from the case. I avoid travel in London wherever possible. The reason I knew this detail about London Bridge was quite a strange one.

Some months before, I found myself on a bench outside of the card shop in London Bridge, passing the time with a Costa coffee and toastie. I was due at an appointment and had arrived early. All that careful journey planning of course. One thing I despise, a strong word yes but I do strongly dislike this, is being late. So, there I was, passing the time.

I noticed the sign in front of me said 'Toliets' instead of 'Toilets'. How can this be so wrong? I wonder who was responsible. No doubt not enough funding to replace a whole sign. Someone obviously had a bad day at work when they realised they had got it wrong. Or have they even realised yet?

Anyway, my previous meeting at London Bridge was in fact an assessment. I had decided to go for an adult autism assessment. I guess I've always been quirky, unique and a little particular with things. This of course isn't enough to assume one is autistic. However, I had personal reasons to consider the possibility and I wanted to embrace whatever the outcome might have been.

It turns out that I didn't meet the benchmark but it was one of the most useful things I've ever done in order to understand myself. No longer did I have a question mark. My anxiety and other ritual behaviours were simply personality traits. I guess this assessment allowed me to like myself and believe in myself. Had the outcome been different would this still be the case? I hope so.

"Okay bye Janet, look forward to seeing you there at 12.30". I was in a hurry now. No longer on my own time zone, I had to plan a new route and stick to timings. I hurried Buddy into the car for his groom.

Pulling up outside 'Top Dog' I decided to check What3words and see the whereabouts of the end of the queue. A message flashed before my eyes, "The queue for the Queen lying in state is now closed. Please do not make your way to Southwark Park".

My heart sank. This can't be true. My snacks were packed, I was ready to do this. What now? I phoned Janet. Not being one to ignore advice I don't know how this happened next but before I knew it I was on the train to London Bridge to meet Janet anyway. We decided we would go and see what was what or as my dad would say 'what's occurring?' Perhaps the queue might open again we thought aloud to each other on the phone. Being British and being told not to join a queue is like being told not to cry at Watership Down. Impossible.

As the carriage rattled along, I wondered if I looked like a typical tourist with my backpack and I felt like everyone knew I was going to see the Queen. If I'm honest I was a bit worried someone was going to tell me off for travelling when we had been told not to. During lockdown when we had to stay at home I didn't even get in the car. 'Stay home saves lives' we were told over and over. So that's what we did. One walk a day as allowed. I'm a rule follower through and through. Maybe it's the teacher in me or maybe it's one of those quirks I mentioned.

Arriving at London Bridge I make my way to the bench outside the card shop. I find myself looking out for the toliet sign. Sure enough there it was. Why had no-one else realised this mistake? Who else had noticed I wonder. Should I report it? To whom? All these thoughts take over as I scan the crowds for pink. Nothing. Just every day commuters going about their business. No one looked like they were going to queue for the Queen. No one looked as guilty as I felt.

I had told Janet to look out for me wearing a dog coat. I, the one who wanted to campaign for parks to be dog free, was actually wearing a coat full of pictures of dogs. I would never have predicted that I would start to enquire about owning a dog in 2019 only to reach the top of the waiting list in 2020. The day I brought Buddy home quite literally changed my life. From dog ignorer to dog lover in a matter of moments. Now I was the proud owner of a dog coat just in case anyone didn't know I loved dogs, this coat would help them. If I had it my way I'd probably have 3 or 4 dogs by now and be a middle aged crazy dog lady. It is Paul and the girls common sense that stops this from happening.

So there I was, sitting in my dog coat, looking out for an aged 60ish lady I'd never met wearing a pink coat. There was only one thing for it, another Costa toastie. Being a creature of habit, I had the same as when I was last at London Bridge and sat in the same seat. It was comforting.

Soon enough, my phone rang. It was Janet! She had been there all along, watching me stuff my face with the toastie no doubt and embarrassingly so. She was holding her coat and it was a reddish colour. I was always a bit too literal; I should have been open to different shades of pink.

"It still says the queue is closed." Janet greeted me.

"Well, we are here now. I just need the toilet first". I wondered how we would manage the queue and toileting and hoped there would be enough facilities. Determined as ever we began to make our way to the underground for the two stops to Southwark Park.

Janet was a natural to get on with from the word go. We chatted and got to know each other on the train.

Disembarking from the surprisingly quiet train, speakers boomed out 'Do not make your way to Southwark Park' over and over. Yet, there were no crowds, it was quite empty. Looking and feeling terribly guilty, we started to do exactly what the tannoy told us not to. We began to make our way to Southwark Park. With all the warnings not to travel and not to go to the park, I was expecting crowds pushing over each other trying to get into the park and felt sure we would be turned away. Maybe the gates will be closed and people are getting squashed. My imagination was playing up. Yet as we approached the park entrance, the gates were wide open and a slow but steady small stream of people were filing through. We hardly dared to speak to each other. We just kept our heads down and quickstepped into Southwark Park.

As we came out of the bushes into the main park, we could see the 'Southwark snake'. Rows upon rows of people queuing in a concertina style fashion. People were walking towards the entrance of the snake, glancing around them as they went. Perhaps everyone, like me, had the guilty feeling for travelling to a closed queue. Stewards shepherded us along past makeshift signs saying '14 hours from this point'. Wow 14 hours, this was the longest queue I had ever seen. I took a photo.

Janet and I held our breaths as we joined the queue. I asked the steward. "Is this the queue queue or the queue for the queue?" Still not quite believing we might be in **THE** queue. "This is the queue queue, you're in it now" came the cheery reply. The time was 1.45pm.

You would think the walk through the concertina railings would be slow and pleasurable as now we were in the queue there was nothing stopping us. However, there was still a sense of urgency by all those around and we walked quickly over metres and metres of black rubber mats. Some of which were trip hazards so I was carefully looking down at my feet. The last thing I wanted was to fall and injure myself. People seemed to be walking past us, rushing to beat us. It led to everyone walking very very quickly. What was the point in being a few people ahead in the queue? It was still 14 hours. Eventually the quick walking stopped and we settled into our place in the queue which had slowed to a standstill. I wonder… Time to start the picnic?

I have always liked my snacks on journeys. As a child, we used to travel in a convoy of four cars down to Spain for a three-week campsite holiday at a place called Camping Cypsela. The two-day journey with an overnight stop in France led to my parents often buying us some new pens and paper and activity books to keep us occupied. No iPads or phones or even DVD players in cars back in the 8O's. Along with the customary stationery came the mint polos.

I remember it being 3.30am, we were just pulling off the drive to catch the early hovercraft over to France and there was a 'crunch' from the back seat (I was in the middle row of the Space Cruiser). My brother David had begun his journey sweets. I think of this as I dig into my bag for a hot cross bun to start the queue journey. If the start is good enough for my brother then it's good enough for me.

Looking around at the people I would be spending the next 14 hours with I was surprised. I'm not even sure why I was surprised. I guess I was expecting some hardened royal fans. Instead, a sea of every day humans faced me. All ages, all genders, all ethnicities and all suitably dressed in trousers, coats and trainers along with backpacks. I was heartened to see some dressed in black dresses and suits. It hadn't occurred to me to dress for a death. How utterly respectful these people were. Some had camping chairs. I wondered would I be jealous of these as time ticked on. It turns out no I wouldn't be. They ended up carrying their chairs all the way and barely sitting on them as no sooner did the queue stop, it then started moving again.

As we edged our way forwards, slowly, step after step, still on the black rubber mats I realised something. This wasn't a queue. This was a very very long slow walk. I was on a journey.

Janet had begun chatting with some ladies behind us. An aunt and two nieces. All the way from Nottingham! I had come all the way from East London and hadn't really expected others to travel from further. My guilt at travelling passed quickly. What if the queue was closed and they had travelled all the way from Nottingham?! My determination was nothing compared to these ladies. A dad and daughter in front of us had travelled from Derbyshire! Wow, people were flocking from everywhere. The two nieces explained that they had got off the coach at Victoria Station and had already walked a great deal of the queue backwards, so they have walked the queue to get to the queue. Honestly you couldn't make this up. Their coach was booked for the next morning at 9am so they planned to just hang about London in the spare hours they were expecting after entering Westminster Hall.

Janet was full blown into a story with the aunt, Karen. They were discussing elderly parents, care and the benefits system. This was all only five minutes into the queue. Although a chatterbox by nature, a true gemini, I'm not one to make small talk to strangers. I walked along with them, mostly quiet, taking in the atmosphere. I wasn't ready to open my heart and soul up.

Whilst in the snake, Janet and I got to know each other a little more. Although we were deemed as two relatives standing together, we had only just met as well. I liked Janet. A lot. She had a warmth to her and was easy to talk to. I enjoyed her company and felt safe having someone there for me. As I'm sure she did for herself.

Janet's mother had recently died. She had been her main carer. A difficult job but one she did with love and care.

We discussed work and children. Janet had never had children. She was close to her nieces and nephews. Something I understand. I have 11 nieces and nephews and love being an auntie as well as a mum to my 2 girls.

News reporters were talking to people in the queue just ahead of us and I wondered if I was going to make it on the news as part of the crowd. They were interviewing under a tree. There were lots of trees I noticed.

I took my jumper off, it was quite warm. Luckily the weather forecast was on our side with dry, average September weather. The sun was shining and it was a lovely late Summer afternoon.

"So I said to my HR, I'm not happy teaching someone permanent all the roles of my job whilst I am freelance. I'm doing myself out of a job".

Janet! My mind had wandered and I hadn't been listening. "I see" I said hoping this would suffice as a relevant response. It did. Janet continued to talk about work for the next 15 minutes. I really wanted to ask what she did but fear I missed that bit at the beginning and couldn't go back. A bit like when you meet someone new, forget their name and then time passes and it's too late to ask. I never did find out. But I did a better job of listening going forwards.

I measured our movement in the queue by keeping my eye on Southwark Park Bandstand. I've seen a few bandstands in my time but never a band playing in one.

Except once, at Kelling Heath holiday park.

It was used as entertainment on those long summer evenings. Firstly the children's entertainer would have all the little ones up on the bandstand to watch the magic tricks. Dave Doughnut not only entertained the kids but the adults too with his jokes and anecdotes. Later in the evening, as the wasps disappeared from the hazy heat of the day, some live music would start up. Oh the Sheringham Shanty Men were fabulous. What a good night that was. I didn't realise I liked a good sea song until I saw the Shanty Men perform. No Shanty Men here though. No Bee Gees or Chris De Burgh either as it felt rude putting in earphones when small talk was on the agenda.

If only the organisation of the queue had included a good old fashioned British Band playing in Southwark Park Bandstand. Now that would have been something. We could have danced along the Southwark snake. Although I'm not sure us Brits would have let our hair down enough to do so. The order of the day was orderly, polite queuing.

Had there been a band it wouldn't have been the first. Music first flowed in Southwark Park in 1878 when the Crown Brass Band was given permission to perform. In 1883, the first wooden bandstand stood proud. By 1889 it was replaced with an iron structure. I could just imagine all the ladies and gentlemen in the park, enjoying a picnic under their summer umbrellas, listening to the live music. The bandstand was demolished in the 1950's after being used as an outdoor classroom and for concerts and dances. It was replicated in 1999 with the help from the Heritage Lottery Fund. How wonderful to keep history alive.

"Why did you decide to join the queue?" We had caught up with the news reporters. What looked like a young couple were answering.

"We saw the queue and we decided we wanted to pay our respects." It was an answer I would hear over and over again. Everyone had the same aim, yet news reporters were fascinated.

"How long have you been queueing so far?" "What time did you join the queue?" The world was fascinated with this queue.

Coming to the end of the Southwark Snake I glanced at my watch. Two hours had passed! Just in Southwark Park. Yet it had gone quickly. Dare I say it, I'd never queued this long before and never enjoyed a queue as much before either. As we walked the home run out of the park stewards either side of us cheered us on.

"Well done", "You've got this", "Keep going". I felt like some kind of hero having achieved something amazing, yet all I had done was queue. I hadn't expected to feel like a marathon runner but it certainly made me feel a sense of achievement and gave a boost of morale to keep going.

It reminded me of when I did a walk for charity years earlier with my friend Marie from school. It was called a 'Strollerthon' and was organised by Cadbury's. As we got to the end of the walk, stewards were congratulating us in much the same way. The only difference was that we were then given out lots of chocolate as we passed the finishing line. Marie and I, not satisfied with a bag full of chocolate then skipped round in a loop and decided to 'finish' the walk for a second time. So once again the stewards congratulated us and we walked through the finish line and got a second bag full of chocolate. The congratulations certainly wasn't deserved on that second occasion. In the same way, they don't really seem deserved having just walked out of Southwark Park.

As we stepped out of the park and into the first road I felt like we were really on our way now. Pavement queuing. This was it, the slow walk that would snake it's way along the South Bank taking us to the Queen lying in state. We were out of the Southwark snake and ready to take on the Thames snake.

As I edged slowly forwards, step by step, hour by hour, landmark by landmark, I thought about all the members of the public that had cheered throughout the years at different royal events. They couldn't all be here now to pay their respects but I could. I felt a deep sense of responsibility, of loyalty, of patriotism. It was over to us. Our generation. To see the Queen to her final resting place in style. Those of us that could queue and were able to queue and had the time to queue represented just about everyone in Britain.

Chapter 4
The Great British Queue

What strikes me on our first bit of road walking is the care and consideration that has gone into the organising of such an event. Okay, so there wasn't a British Band playing in Southwark Park but as we walk slowly along Cathay Street, which involves crossing a road, stewards are there helping us to cross safely. This is not only the longest queue I have ever been in, but it is the most orderly. Just how we like it.

Us Brits love to queue they say. This stems from the war, queueing for rations. In order to hold back the frenzy, it was advertised that queueing in an orderly manner was a British trait and we must be proud to be British. Hence the expression 'no-one queues like the British.' A few foreign holidays abroad have led me to believe this statement is in fact highly correct.

As the afternoon sun creeps through the clouds the queue comes to life. People begin walking ahead of the queue then walking back past us with pints and cokes and crisps in their hands. Now I understand how the queue works. It was beginning to make sense. We could leave the queue and vary off it slightly. As long as we find our way back to our place in the queue. Everyone knows and recognises the people in front and behind them at this point, so queue hijacking seems unlikely.

A break in the heads in front of me signals a joyful sight. A pub. Ah so this is where the food and drinks are coming from. The Angel Pub. Not any pub but the first pub out of many that we would pass as we snake along the riverbank.

The Angel pub was built in 1830 with some reports saying it incorporates part of a 17th century building. The perfect spot overlooking the Thames. Previously the pub had stood on the opposite corner, dating back even further to the 16th century. Legend would say that Captain Cook frequented The Angel on the Thames. I look up and read the large sign on the corner of the pub:

'The Angel, re-built c. 1837

in it's present form is by far

the oldest tavern sign

in Rotherhithe. It is recorded in the 17th century and may go back to the middle ages. The Angel was once sited diagonally opposite, alongside the moat of King Edward III's mansion, but has long stood on the riverfront next to Rotherhithe or Redriffe stairs.

Thinking about the history of the Angel pub I consider the local pub I frequented as a young adult. The Monkhams in Buckhurst Hill. I used to make £1 last all evening by getting five blackcurrant and soda's. So did my cousin Martine. They were 17p each. The soda was free. I bet they loved us in there. I make a mental note to visit again sometime soon and see what I can get with a pound.

Slightly jealous of those brave enough to run ahead and get drinks (no blackcurrant and soda in sight) and then find their way back to the queue, I busy myself chatting with Janet and making plans in case we have to leave the queue.

"I've got a bright pink umbrella with me." I knew it would come in handy when I packed it despite no forecast for rain.

"I'll put it up if you need to leave the queue so you can find me again."

"I was thinking the same. It's why I wore my pink coat." Janet and I were enjoying finding our common ground. Planning was one of them.

On our left we pass some old wall ruins.

"I wonder what used to be there" I say aloud. No one seems to know. I check my maps on my mobile phone whilst trying to conserve my battery power as much as possible. I found out that the ruins were once a royal dwelling. King Edward III's Manor House.

The Manor House was built in 1350 at a time when the Thames boundaries were different and flooded further inland than today. His Manor House stood on a small island, surrounded by a moat as a display of status and also protection. It is believed that the river marshes provided the perfect spot for his hobby of being a falconer.

I imagine the road we are walking on as marshy river water and I wonder what King Edward III would make of this queue almost 700 years after his reign.

King Edward III came to the throne aged just 14 and held a 50 year reign. He is best known for starting the 100 years war with France. Seeing the ruin walls and grassland I wonder what else there is of archaeological significance on the site that is yet to be found. Surely some long lost treasures are hidden beneath. Alas, we will not be the ones to find out. A sign as clear as mud states:

'For your safety please take care as historic sights can be hazardous. Children should be kept under close control. Willful damage to the monument is an offence. Unauthorised use of metal detectors is prohibited'.

Being an avid fan of 'The Detectorists' Paul would enjoy this history and yet be disappointed at not being able to find the treasure that he is convinced is all around us and underneath us.

I bought him a metal detector a few years ago. It's hard to find places where he can metal detect besides public beaches that allow it. I think the extent of his findings so far have been a couple of coins that I myself have thrown into the sand for him to find. Still, this doesn't stop him looking and acting the part, walking up and down the beach as I watch from Bertie or Bettie Boutique Beach Huts, a hired beach hut in Gorleston-on-sea.

Talking of huts, the first set of portaloos are in a row alongside the Angel Pub. Some facing towards the queue. Some facing the Thames. The time has come to leave the queue for the first time.

Looking again at the people in front and behind me and ensuring Janet has her pink jacket on, I quick step along the queue to the toilets. Deciding the ones facing the queue are a bit risky in case of door lock failure I venture to the other side. What a beautiful day it was turning out to be. Blue sky and sunshine and the Thames looking vibrant and busy. I take my first selfie.

The portaloo experience was to be expected. Knees touching the door and dark inside. However, it was very clean and toilet roll in abundance. No need for my tissue supplies here. As I was sitting on the toilet facing the door leading out to the Thames I giggled to myself. I felt like Caractacus Potts father from the film Chitty Chitty Bang Bang. The scene where he is in a small hut and gets lifted off across the land and sea singing "The posh posh travelling life, the travelling life for me." Let's hope that doesn't happen here and when I step out I'm still on solid ground by the River Thames.

As luck would have it, it wasn't my day for that kind of an adventure. However, as I disembark from the portaloo, I find myself face to face with a statue of a man sitting on a bench, wearing a hat and glasses and leaning on an umbrella. As I look around there is also a statue of a girl, a cat and a lady. I say lady as she looks the part although she is leaning on a shovel. Delighted to find a plaque, it tells me 'Dr Salters Daydream by Diane Gorvin 1991 for London Docklands'. Dr Salters Daydream? This sounds interesting and I love how the statues are placed as though living in a real life scene. I've never seen anything like it before.

It turns out the scene depicted was rather sad. The artist was depicting Dr Salter sitting in his old age imagining happier times with his daughter Joyce playing. Sadly, Joyce had died aged only eight years old.

Dr Salter (1873-1945) and his wife Ada were much loved figures in Bermondsey and Rotherhithe. He worked as a doctor, helping the poorest of patients without charge. His idea was to improve the people's health regardless of wealth. This was before the National Health Service was established. His wife worked with working women, improving conditions and fighting for rights. She became the first woman councillor in Bermondsey and the first woman mayor in London. She also promoted environmental projects. Sadly, their work amongst the poor and most vulnerable led to their daughter's death from scarlet fever. What an uplifting yet sad tale.

Right, back to reality and now time to find Janet. I glance back to where we had been in the queue and scan the queue for signs of our crew. They have gone ahead. When I catch up with them, despite seeing many others rejoin the queue, I still have an element of concern that people might think I'm a queue jumper.

Luckily I am welcomed with open arms. David and Laura, the father and daughter that are in the queue with us gesture to me to get back in line. I say 'with us' as we were slowly becoming one group. This would prove very important later on as we 'left the queue' for half an hour! More on that later.

David and Laura had travelled down from Derbyshire. Both were so respectful to the occasion that they changed into black at the end of the queue before entering the Queen lying in state in Westminster Hall. Laura his daughter is an avid Queen fan. Not 'We will rock you' type Queen but of course the Queen we are in the queue for. When news broke that the Queen had died, she told us that her friends and colleagues all checked in with her to make sure she was ok. This wasn't just a sausage roll and cup of tea at royal celebrations type of respect but a different level. I noticed throughout the walk, she was relatively quiet, deep in thought and eager to get to the front of the queue.

Out of all the 'gang crew' it was David that would stay in touch, with texts at the Queen's funeral, the King's first Christmas speech and the King's coronation. Royal events would take on a new meaning in my life. Time to connect again with Janet and David. David called me Laura Q. I liked it. In return his name is stored in my phone as David Q.

We continue with our slow walk through Bermondsey Wall East. The sense of community is uplifting and I'm not talking about the people in the queue. Makeshift tables are set up with hot water urns and tea, coffee and biscuits are being given out. The strange realisation for me was that I didn't want to join the queue of approximately six people for a cup of tea. It seemed long. Yes I was in a queue of thousands but it didn't feel like a queue. It felt like a slow walk, a pilgrimage perhaps?

The definition of pilgrimage is a journey to a place of spiritual or religious significance. It isn't simply visiting somewhere. Tourists of Rome aren't pilgrims but those that journey together to Rome are. We were journeying together in the queue to see the Queen. Had we just walked straight into Westminster Hall I doubt the spiritual impact would have been felt. It would have simply been a visit.

This was a journey. I do not feel like I am in a queue. Four people in front of me at Tesco's feels longer than this queue. I'm not about to join another queue within the queue.

All this changed some time later when the queues for the toilets got longer and I would have no choice but to 'queue outside of the queue'.

Just around the corner from the tea urn stalls, once everyone is satisfied and full up with tea and biscuits, we come across Fountain Green Square. A lovely setting of townhouses overlooking the Thames. Some children are selling home made cakes and serving tea.

I feel for them as lots of queuers have already utilised both the Angel pub and the refreshments set up around the previous corner. I don't buy anything from the children but if I had my time again, I would have. Just to help them with a customer. They would remember forever the days they made cakes for the Queen's Queue. It was heartening.

Continuing on through the Southwark Estate I manage another selfie with the queue behind me. Just then someone opens their windows from the River View Heights complex and shouts 'God save the King'. Everyone in the queue is so British in the sense of wary of excitement or noise so they mostly ignore the man shouting. I hoped we would all cheer but the focus was on the queue, one step in front of the other, no distractions, not even for the King.

The first opportunity to sit down comes at the end of Mill Street. Just past the Co-op there are some long steps and if you peer over them there is a lovely sight of the river between the wharf buildings. The queue comes momentarily to a standstill. I sit down. Having queued for over four hours at this point I let my legs stretch out in front of me taking the weight off my feet. It feels good.

Until I have to stand up again. Ouch. Now my feet hurt. Having been diagnosed with plantar fasciitis in the weeks before joining the queue I have support arches in my trainers. They are doing the trick but I certainly feel it when standing after sitting.

In order to sit for a little longer next time, if I saw a bench or wall I walked ahead to sit and slowly watched the walking queue go past, waved at Janet and then quickstepped to catch up as she disappeared into the distance. Strangely Janet, a good 20 years older than me, didn't feel the need to sit. There was one glorious moment of the queue where there was a wall bench that stretched along the Thames for what seemed like a long time where most people stopped walking and bum shuffled along the wall instead.

My next opportunity to sit came just a short while later as we passed multiple wharf buildings. Cinnamon Wharf thank you. Some wonderful steps for tired feet to rest. The good part of the Cinnamon Wharf steps was that as Janet passed me I could just hop along to the other steps as it was a double entry staircase, allowing me to sit for double the time. I glanced in at the receptionist working inside the building and couldn't work out if it was offices or accommodation.

Turns out accommodation. A two bed flat for the neat price of £1.3 million. Moving on.

Shad Thames next. For those that have never walked along Shad Thames it reminds me of something out of Oliver Twist. I can just imagine the busy market scene of people moving their wares around. It is actually a typical docklands street that has survived redevelopment. With tall warehouses on either side and iron bridges crossing the warehouses, it allowed dockers to pass goods from the Thames through to warehouses inland. The dockers would also wait and hope to get work in the warehouse.

As the queue walks slowly through Shad Thames there is an abundance of shops, restaurants, offices and hairdressers. One in particular takes my fancy. La Pont de la Tour. A restaurant and wine merchant. Bottles and bottles of wine are on the other side of the window as we shuffle past with our backpacks and sandwiches. As we approach the end of Shad Thames, a multitude of queuers leave the queue for Starbucks. Either for the refreshments or toilets. I'm not sure.

I find myself fancying a coffee. It would help keep me awake. However, I soon bury the idea. I don't want to upset my tummy on this queue which coffee can be known to do. I need to keep my toileting needs to a minimum. So, no coffee for me. We plod on, past the Anchor Brewhouse and reach the end of Shad Thames.

Having dipped down away from the Thames, passing Queen Elizabeth Street no less, Mill Street, Shad Thames and St. Saviours Dock, we now found ourselves back along the Thames riverfront and right in front of us is Tower Bridge. Despite being a Londoner, the sight was pretty breathtaking. I leave the queue with one of the nieces behind us and we take a photo of each other to remember the wow moment we have just experienced.

Looking at Tower Bridge is like looking at history itself. You feel time warped back to the past of dungeons and dragons. Okay so maybe not dragons but I'm sure you get what I mean. It looks like there are mini castles on the bridge itself.

Designed by Sir Horace Jones and Sir John Wolfe Barry in 1884, construction began in 1886 and the bridge was completed after eight years in 1894. Queen Victoria signed the Tower Bridge Act giving permission for its build. Her son the Prince of Wales lay the first stone. However, it was to be 114 years before a King or Queen visited inside Tower Bridge. Queen Elizabeth II was the first and currently only monarch to visit those that worked inside the bridge. Good for her.

As we edge past the bridge a police officer is posing for selfies with some children from the queue. He lets them wear his hat. I am pleased there isn't a new world policy in place stopping this joyous moment for these children. I am tempted to ask for a selfie myself but not being a child, trying to conserve my battery etc., all leads to me observing from a distance instead.

This wasn't the only time I would be observing the police closely in the queue. As time ticked on we came across an abandoned bag in a doorway of a building. I was pleased that I wasn't the only one concerned. We were, after all, in a now famous queue in the middle of London. David Q told a nearby steward who started talking on his phone. I don't think even a minute had passed when police officers arrived to check out the bag. We all stood back as one brave police officer checked out the contents. A packed lunch. Whoever's bag it was, well, what a poor sod. All organised and ready for the queue then they lose their bag on a rest break.

Talking of poor sods, an American theme park bought the old London Bridge and when they assembled it back together they were surprised. They had mistaken Tower Bridge for London Bridge and thought they were buying Tower Bridge. They probably thought they had quite the bargain.

Chapter 5
Wristbands

The riskiest part of the queue, where there might be queue hijackers, was just past Tower Bridge. As we go under the bridge, the queue begins moving quickly and gaps begin to form between people. It is a busy Friday evening and the time is now 7pm. We have been queueing for just over four hours. I have enjoyed every minute. I'm not usually a people watcher but I am realising fast that I am a building and sight watcher aka sightseer.

As we make our way across the crowds trying to keep up with the queue a wonderful sight greeted us. Wristbands! I had forgotten about these but had heard about them when watching the news about the queue. I wondered how many people had simply jumped the queue at this stage and skipped a whole four hours! We step up the pace to ensure the gaps between us and the people ahead is as small as it could be. A queue hijacker at this point would be most unwelcome. The thought of it is making me tense and a bit panicky. I don't want someone to get in front of me that shouldn't be. It feels a bit like when you are the last person in the queue at a buffet. There is nothing worse. Seeing all the lovely food being taken and enjoyed by those in front of you, hoping against hope that there will be enough delights left for your own plate. For me my eye is always on the chicken satay and coronation chicken sandwiches.

Although I suffer with buffet panic I must admit that there has always been enough of the food I want. Perhaps it is evolution working at its best. Food to survive. Our brains sometimes don't realise the difference between now and years ago, danger versus non danger or dare I say it, greed.

Queue hijackers clear, we line up to get our wristbands. The giving out of wristbands is a little chaotic compared to the rest of the queue. Stewards are handing them out willy nilly in no particular order. We just have to push our way to the steward to make sure we get one. They make sure we put it on in front of them, which leads to mine not being quite as perfectly stuck on as one would have hoped. It is orange, everyone's seemed to be. What I find a little strange and eerie was that the number on the wristband was very similar to my date of birth. What are the chances? It has a serial number and at quick glance I honestly feel like I am looking at my birthday.

The numbers on the wristband do not mean anything to us in relation to the queue. The numbers aren't in any particular order to those around me. There is no 'number in the queue' with the number above behind me and the number below in front of me. I had thought we would have to queue in a set order but there was none of that. The wristband was simply proof we were in the queue. They were checked once or twice along the queue so that was reassuring.

I must admit to not loving wristbands. At places of interest, for example, zoo's, theme parks and the like, I try not to put them on when given them. My preference is to just keep in my pocket and hope I'm not asked to put it on. In contrast my girls love a wristband! In fact they would go out of their way to get one and take selfies with it. I think it's the festival culture amongst the youth today. A wristband symbolises moments of fun.

Anyway, with regards to the queue wristband I do feel a little more relaxed now that I have it. I feel that no one would be able to deny my place now. It feels a little like the euphoria at joining the queue in

Southwark Park and again after finishing the Southwark Snake. Receiving the wristband is certainly a queue milestone. The wristband states: LISQ, 'Lying in state queue'. It also says 'This wristband does not guarantee entry and is strictly non-transferable'. It may not guarantee entry but I still have at least 36 hours before the queue closes so I am reassured that my entry is as guaranteed as it can be at this stage.

Just as I am admiring my wristband I see something looming ahead of us. The Tower Bridge snake. More queuing barriers on the green looking back at Tower Bridge. Another hour of snaking up and down, feeling as though no progress is being made but forever looking back at the beginning of the snake and feeling grateful not to be there. More portaloos meaning people going under the railings of the snake to catch up with their crew. Janet's turn this time. The queue feels like it is moving quickly whilst Janet isn't there. I have to keep my eye on the portaloos and wave frantically as Janet appears over the lines of people. Alongside our queue people are walking fast beside us and overtaking to catch up with their family and friends. This is now part of the queue norm. As long as no one stops in front of us then there is no suspicion. It really is the most civilised of queues. This is the queue we had all been in training for our whole lives. The Great British Queue. One news reporter captured it perfectly.

"It is a moment for which Britain has been in solemn preparation for years. Multiple official agencies were brought together. Meticulous plans were secretly drawn up. Intricate logistical technicalities were ironed out. A route was carefully mapped out.

And no country's population could have been better prepared for it.

We are talking, of course, about the queue which Britons must join in order to pay their respects to Queen Elizabeth II. This is not an ordinary line. It has taken on symbolic meaning, a ritual to be undertaken, an embodiment of the national mood. It is, in short, The Queue" CNN Ivana Kottasova September 15th 2022.

'A ritual to be undertaken' resonated with me. It certainly felt like something I just had to do. I was compelled from the first moments the queue began to form. As were 250,000 others.

Back to the snake and the sights across the Thames are enough to keep me occupied during the Tower Bridge snake. I am reminded of the Olympics in 2012 when the opening ceremony had a sketch of the Queen and James Bond flying into the arena. At one point they flew through Tower Bridge. It is funny how most of what we are seeing in the queue has a link to royalty in one way or another.

Looking beyond the sea of heads in front of me I can take in the sights of both the Tower of London and Tower Bridge. Both are looking stunning as the sun is setting. The Tower of London always connotates prisoners, executions, hung, drawn and quartered style stories. It is, however, officially a royal palace. The rumour is if the ravens leave the palace, the monarchy will fall. I believe the ravens wings are clipped to avoid such catastrophe. If they weren't clipped would they make their hasty escape I wonder? Is there any truth to the rumour? Hopefully the clipping of wings prevents us from finding out.

My thoughts are broken by Janet ushering me into a huddle. Time for our first and only group photo in the Tower Bridge snake. I end up in the middle of the photo acting the part of British queuer. By this time I have my jumper on and my dog coat. Layers are proving handy as I suspected they would.

Sunning ourselves in Southwark Park seems quite some time ago now. Five hours have passed. I was certain we were going to make it in about eight hours as the queue was constantly moving. It turns out that I am wrong by about four hours. It ended up taking 12 hours or half a day or 720 minutes or 43,200 seconds. Either way, it was 12 hours that I am lest to forget.

As we queue, once again on the rubber mats, as was now custom for the snaking, there is someone with a wheely suitcase. Well. The noise I'll never forget. Up and down, up and down, the wheels go over the rubber. Fellow queuers begin letting the owner past them, as do we, and the owner and case soon disappear into the distant sunset. Anything not to have that noise going on and on and on. It was really annoying repetitive noise and it wasn't just me thinking this. Our whole group are also talking about the wheely noise. Thinking about it now, I will have to consider taking a case if ever I queue like this again. It's a sure fire way of getting to the front more quickly.

As we make our way towards the last few lines of the snake it feels good. Another achievement, another snake. Tick. Done. Getting there. I look on my queue tracker. The queue is still backed up to Southwark Park. It feels good to have five hours under our belt. Janet is still chatting away. I am more than happy to listen. I also share some stories. We are good company for each other.

As we 'disembark' from the snake we find ourselves creeping along the side of the Thames up to HMS Belfast. Why have I never visited before? I feel like not only am I queueing but I am having a lovely sightseeing day out in London. The difference is that I can't just pop in and visit places like one might if they were a sightseer. The mental notes list of revisiting places in the queue is getting longer. As we pigeon step one foot in front of the other there is plenty of time to read the signs and find out more. This would simply have to do for now.

Just outside of HMS Belfast I begin to read:

'There's no ship quite like HMS Belfast. HMS Belfast is Britain's most significant surviving warship from the Second World War. Since Belfast's launch in 1938, it has fought in the Arctic, fired some of the first shots on D-Day and seen major action during the Korean War'. At the bottom of the sign it says IWM, Imperial War Museums.

Imperial War Museum. Now there's a memory. As a child, my parents took us to Duxford Imperial War Museum and I remember thinking it was the best day out ever. EVER. I don't remember the planes. However, there was a prefab set up outside with windows to peer in the different rooms. It was set up as though it was the war. I loved looking through those windows. I can remember the old fashioned feeling I got. I could imagine living in the house during the war. There was a bowl under the bed for toileting. I found it fascinating. It began a love of history in my life. Strangely I never studied history after the age of 14. I didn't choose it for GCSE or A Level and I often wonder why.

I drag my children around castles and places of historical interest and museums thinking that they must love this just like I loved the prefab at Duxford. I'm not sure they do.

Luckily I married someone who also likes to imagine history. It is also the prefab bedroom at Duxford that led to a life long love of old fashioned clothes. I have never braved embracing that in public like the time warp wives I sometimes watch on the internet but I am susceptible to an old white cotton nightie. (Sorry Paul) There used to be a shop called Past Times and I loved getting nightwear from there and getting into bed as though I was in the war in the prefab. I'm fascinated by those that choose to live in different centuries even in the modern day. It's probably just a consequence of circumstances that I didn't ever go down this route.

I often search jobs as visitor assistants that need to dress up in Victorian gear or similar. I think it would be quite the perfect role for me! Perhaps one day, when it's time to retire, I might go for a volunteer role with English Heritage or National Trust. I think it would be right up my street.

Right, back in the moment, we are passing HMS Belfast. It is bigger than I thought! I try to imagine life on it during the war. It's very hard to do so. I wouldn't wish to go back in time and be on the warship at all. It takes some level of bravery to be in the Navy or Army. I don't think I'm built to run towards danger. I'm often on the look out for it in every day life ready to run or plan an escape if needed. I used to think I would make a fantastic risk assessor as I used to see danger everywhere. However, I was put straight on that when someone said that I would actually make a very bad risk assessor due to not having realistic probabilities. I always used to think worst case scenarios would happen. I am pleased to say that this level of worry is no longer a major feature of my life, although of course, as a mum, I have my worries. Talking of which, the security issue of thousands queuing in London did cross my mind a few times. Luckily, with Janet to chat to, the worry didn't last long and was out of my thoughts as soon as it was in them.

I can only imagine the hardship HMS Belfast has seen. Being only one of three surviving ships from D Day, it took on the injured and it's crew scanned the beaches once the fighting had died down to search for survivors. If only ships could talk.

I've lived some history of D Day through my parents interest in the war. I remember in particular Pegasus Bridge in France, where British soldiers parachuted in to seize the village in the early hours of D Day. I remember being taken there and feeling the history around me. I've also spent time in Ypres, Belgium where there are various museums and memorials in relation to the First World War. Learning about history in the place it took place takes on a whole different level of understanding and respect. I have vowed to take my children to Ypres but haven't got there yet.

Wages on the HMS Belfast were on the poverty line with only 21 shillings paid per week, slightly more if you were married and more again if you had children. In August 1963 she was saved from destruction thanks to the Imperial War Museum and became a harbour ship, opening to the public in October 1971. A wonderful opportunity for historical learning to take place.

Suddenly, a place to sit down! The stone wall running along the Thames has a bench built into it the length of the wall. Perfect! We all start bum shuffling along. Again, Janet stood. What a woman! I was taking every chance I could. Darkness was beginning to draw in and it is time for my woolly hat to keep the chill off. We enjoy a good amount of time seated. The nieces use small camping stools to sit on. They are proving useful every so often. Much better than the bigger, normal sized camping chairs which aren't worth getting out of the bags as by the time you do, the queue is moving again. There are a few people with them though but I haven't seen them made good use of yet. Just another thing to carry.

As we come out of the 'bum shuffling wall' we come across Hay's Galleria. A wonderful assault on the senses with colour, smells and lights in abundance. Originally part of the Hay's Wharf, built in the mid 1850's, to house tea clippers from India and China, Hay's Galleria stands on the same spot where the tea clippers did all those years ago. Visiting today you'll find a choice of eateries, market stalls and souvenirs. Ideally located between Tower Bridge and London Bridge, perfect for an afternoon browse.

Not today though, onwards we walk, united with our one aim in mind. To pay our respects to the late Queen Elizabeth II. Not only pay our respects but say thank you. Thank you for a life of service to us. A life of commitment and dedication to people the world over. Will we ever have such a fantastic long reigning monarch again? Certainly not one that we will ever know of in our lifetime. Public appearances until the week she died. She clearly put the monarchy first before any personal needs. A true and great modern sacrifice story.

Even more remarkable is the fact that she should never have been Queen in the first place. Her uncle, King Edward VIII was the rightful heir and became King in January 1936. However, he wasn't to reign for very long. There was a key aspect of his private life that did not fit in with the British Monarchy. He was in love with an American divorcee. As the King of England is also the head of the Church of England, this caused some problems. His wife would not be recognised as Queen. Edward came up with a solution. Why not give her a lesser title and any children will not be heirs to the throne? In effect, he was happy to stay as King and accept that his immediate family reign would end with himself. Winston Churchill was also happy with this arrangement but alas when put to the British Cabinet, the idea was rejected.

King Edward VIII abdicated from the throne in December 1936. He chose love. Elizabeth's father George became King George VI.

Just over 15 years later, aged just 24, Elizabeth became Queen when her father died whilst she was in Kenya. Her son Charles, first in line to the throne for 70 years, became King upon the Queen's death in 2022. Long live the King.

Leaving Hay's Galleria full of life behind us, and HMS Belfast now dark and empty, with the sun setting next to it, we find ourselves at London Bridge. Now there's a story to tell. Did you know it used to hold 140 houses in the late 14th century?

Chapter 6
Bridge Houses

I wasn't wowed by London Bridge. I think I would probably quite easily have made the same mistake as the American theme park owners. When I think of London Bridge, it's an image of Tower Bridge that comes to mind. The current London Bridge is obviously a wonderful design and practical for the amount of traffic passing over it daily. Aesthetically? It's nothing very exciting. Especially when you've just passed Tower Bridge with the Tower of London in the background.

What does make London Bridge stand out is the Shard building at London Bridge station. Rising 72 floors high it dominates the local landscape with its shops, restaurants, office space and soon to be living space. A relatively new building, having completed work in July 2012. As far as modern buildings go, I feel it fits in with the series of various architectural types along the Thames. We march on past London Bridge when one of our group (I can't remember who) strikes up another conversation.

"Did you know people used to have houses on London Bridge?"

"Houses? How did they have houses on it? Did they live in them?" I found myself replying.

"Oh yes, at its maximum, 140 houses were on London Bridge"

Now that was a piece of history I hadn't known before. Of course, without my history GCSE, it wasn't the only piece of history I didn't know. There are so many gaps in my historical knowledge. Too many. I must do something about that and read a little more widely.

Looking out at the grey, dark, traffic filled bridge, I can hardly dare to imagine the people living on it 700 years ago. I don't think I've ever heard of people living on bridges before. It sounds a bit risky to me. I wonder what the people looked like and what their lives were like. I wonder if any of their spirits are still around.

Someone once told me that half the people you see in London are actually ghosts. Has anyone else heard this? Is it true? When I am travelling on the tube I sit and look and try to guess which people are the ghosts. Sometimes I think it's obvious. Other times, a little harder. Is it the old fashioned looking man with a dusty looking suit? Or the old lady with a shawl? Luckily I've never come across one like the one in Ghost the film where he shouts 'Get off my train'. A bit of a scary untoward character.

The ghosts I think I might see don't scare me. In fact, when I could possibly be amongst the dead I feel most at peace. For example, walking around graveyards. It is surprisingly comforting. All those buried around me have somehow experienced death, the least I can do is read their headstone and remember them. Paul quite enjoys this activity too. The girls I'm not so sure about but we generally don't get any complaints when we pull them into another church cemetery we might be passing when on our holidays.

My favourite one is St. Anne's Church, Over Haddon. A typical village church and graveyard. I imagine the lives of the people that lay buried. I am pleased to honour their memory by taking the time to read their inscription aloud and discuss who they might have been with the girls. Paul has suggested I write a book linking all the gravestones together to tell their intertwined lives. Never say never.

I actually miss the next ten minutes of the queue as I keep looking back to London Bridge, imagining life gone by. I would love to close my eyes and be in the past. So many good things about the past, yet so much illness and disease. I wonder if we will ever be able to go back in the past? I started reading a book recently called 'A Briefer History of Time' by Stephen Hawkings. Let's be honest, his actual book, 'A Brief History of Time', would be far too intellectual for me. I went for the easier option. It's still a difficult read, yet fascinating. I am still absorbing the first chapter before I can go on to the next and it's been a few months now. Surely time travel is possible or will be in the not too distant future.

In my philosophy class we speak about the possibility of there being a 'simultaneous presence being' without time. No past, present or future. All time happening simultaneously. No future, no past. Just everything at once. I wonder if this is true and time is just a human concept.

I think time and space are concepts that we will never fully understand as mere humans. Physicians these days have a particularly tough job with all the new knowledge out there. Rather them than me. (Note: If you are interested in the philosophy of time with a theological twist I recommend you read about Boethius' watcher on the hill or Anselm's four dimensional approach.)

Anyway, I indulge myself, watching imaginary families coming in and out of their homes on London Bridge in the 14th century. I start to wonder whether reincarnation is true and if it is, did I ever live on London Bridge? Would I have been rich or poor? Happy or sad? I look at it with fascination.

It wasn't the London Bridge I was looking at that used to hold houses. The current London Bridge was built in 1971 and is known as the modern bridge. Opened on March 17th 1973 by our very own Queen Elizabeth II. Before this there was the Victorian stone arch bridge built in 1832.

For almost 700 years prior to this, stood the medieval stone arch bridge from 1176-1832. This is the bridge that had houses on it. It stood 150 metres east of the current bridge. I look to the flowing river east of the bridge and wonder what treasures lay beneath. The bridge had nineteen arches, a wooden drawbridge and the river flowed with force underneath.

Two names associated with the building of the bridge are Peter of Colechurch and Isembert of Saintes. Both experienced in their trade with Peter having rebuilt an earlier wooden London Bridge and

Isembert having been involved in building bridges with houses on them in France. Together they built a bridge that lasted 700 years. It is hard to imagine with our throw away and replace culture today.

Although common to live on medieval bridges in Europe, London Bridge was by far the longest. In 1695, 551 people lived on the bridge. It was like a town within the city. People lived on the bridge, people died on the bridge. What amazing stories there must be to tell.

Leases passed on through the families, resulting in some people living their whole life on the bridge. Imagine spending all of your years living on London Bridge in the 17th century or even earlier.

Tenants had to pay an entry fine to begin living on the bridge and then yearly rent. Many leases ended by death, bankruptcy or changing circumstances.

The 'Bridge House' retained ownership and kept records of rent and administration relating to the bridge. It was organised and fair.

There is a story of a clothworkers daughter living on the bridge with her family. She fell from a window into the river. The clothworkers apprentice jumped in to save her and the clothworker was eternally grateful. Eventually he allowed his daughter to marry her saviour.

Other suitors were interested but he believed his apprentice was most deserving of the privilege.

In 1578, L. Grenade from France said of the bridge;

"a great and powerful bridge, the most magnificent that exists in the whole of Europe. It is... completely covered with houses which are all like big castles. And the shops are great storehouses full of all sorts of very opulent merchandise. And there is nowhere in London which is more commercial than this bridge ... I reiterate that there is no bridge in the whole of Europe which is on a great river like the Thames and as formidable, as spectacular and as bustling with trade as this bridge in London."

People flocked from all over to buy and sell on London Bridge. Buildings accommodated both homes and commercial premises, linked together.

The houses on the bridge were two storeys to begin with but soon grew to be three and four storeys high. The rebuilding of them was constant due to disrepair or fire. Unlike the bridge itself which survived so much. At the end of the 17th century all the houses were rebuilt.

Shops were on the ground floor of the houses with living quarters above. Inventories of premises were held at the 'Bridge House' and included counters, cupboards and drawers. Various trades were documented, including, scrivener, milliner, glover, draper, hosier, girdler, mercer, fletcher, vintner, ironmonger, skinner and salter. However, it was the trade of haberdashers that dominated the bridge. Grocers began to appear and sell various spices and metal. Eventually the 17th century saw clockmakers, trunkmakers, bookshops and coffee houses.

Food and drink didn't feature for centuries before this due to the fire risk of ovens. The new coffee houses were popular and some might say continue to be in the area today.

Pedlars were also known to buy from London Bridge. In 1694, it is documented that a Humphrey Searel was imprisoned for selling apples on London Bridge. Poor old Humphrey. I wonder what his story is and what led to him selling apples. Also, what became of him once he was imprisoned? I have no doubt he ended up in the locally placed Clink Prison.

The houses were not only known for their commercial aspects on the ground floor but also for being 'cross houses'. This means houses merged on the first, second and third floor across the bridge creating mini tunnels for those travelling through the bridge. The cross houses were usually every other house, allowing for light to enter the bridge street. I think they would probably be called 'link detached' today although they were terraced along the bridge and then link detached with the opposite house via the upper floors. Maybe 'terrace linked' is a better phrase. Do search for pictures and have a look for yourself.

The kitchens had trapdoors so that water could be raised from buckets from the river below. Eventually in later build houses, pumps were used. I wonder how it was living with these with families and small children. I certainly wouldn't fancy raising children on a bridge that had trapdoors in my home leading to strong tidal water below.

The water would have been used for cooking and cleaning. At least they didn't have to pay water rates.

The houses were made of timber. This was the best material as it meant minimal weight on the bridge. However, significant buildings such as the Stone Gate and Drawbridge Tower were made with stone.

The living quarters were small, with beds being recorded as being in the main hall and sometimes in the shop itself. Can you imagine living and working in a shop on London Bridge and sleeping in the shop each day as well? I always see people of the past as hard grafters. I'm not sure if I'm right or not. There must have been some lazy people too but I just don't think many people in history had the choice in the past. It was either work hard and survive and be fed or face the consequences. If that meant sleeping in your shop after a days trade then so be it.

Key buildings on the bridge included the Chapel, Gatehouse and Drawbridge Tower. The chapel was a place of pilgrimage for travellers. Peter of Colechurch was buried there. An honour after being involved in the building of the bridge.

The chapel was rebuilt by Henry Yevele in the late 14th century after fire. The rebuild included stairs on the outside of the chapel so that people could arrive by boat, allowing even more pilgrim visitors. It was dedicated to St. Thomas Becket originally. However, when he was declared a traitor it was rededicated to St. Thomas the Apostle. Eventually, the Chapel became a private dwelling in 1556 and was the largest house on the bridge. I think if it was still there and up for sale

I might be tempted! A chapel on London Bridge sounds like a pretty good place to live to me. I can only imagine it's worth if it still stood today.

The Gatehouse was known as Stone Gate and defended London against various rebellions. The Drawbridge Tower also helped to defend London and provided practical passageway to ships. The tower had four corner towers, known to have poles on that displayed executed heads. Most notably William Wallace in 1305. I close my eyes and imagine this old bustling bridge, now no longer. If I could ever work out time travel, with Stephen Hawking's help, this is where I would like to go. A life on the bridge. Maybe I should finish my 'Briefer History of Time' book in case it gives any hints as to how to go about it.

At each end of the bridge were public toilets for travellers and those without toilets in their houses. I can't say I would want to travel back in time to see those. Apparently at one point they consisted of long wooden planks with holes in. Was there any privacy? Did you just sit next to someone on the next available hole? I would like to think that surely some discreet system of walls were in place.

In 1665, residents of the bridge were mostly unaffected by the plague. It has been said that perhaps the air flow from the river helped to blow the germs away. As we know today, air flow is important in helping not to spread diseases. Maybe during our recent pandemic of Covid 19 we should have all set up camp on one of the London Bridges.

Fire in 1633, 1666 and 1725 led to many repairs being needed. It is no wonder that eventually it was decided to remove all the houses on London Bridge.

The road became narrow for traffic and insurance companies were reluctant to insure houses on the bridge. As well as that, new bridges were being built. Westminster Bridge opened in 1750 and Blackfriars Bridge in 1769. So in 1757 all houses and leases were bought back and the removal of houses began. I feel for those that had long term leases from generation to generation. There must have been some reluctant evictees.

The bridge survived another 70 years with no houses on it before being destroyed in 1832. This followed the completion of the rebuild next to it, designed by John Rennie.

I hum to myself 'London Bridge is falling down, falling down, falling down. London Bridge is falling down. My fair lady'. It turns out this nursery rhyme wasn't created when the bridge was destroyed in 1832 but had been around for some centuries in various forms. More sinister interpretations of the rhyme point to the use of a medieval punishment known as 'immurement', which is where someone is locked up in a room until they die. 'Take the key and lock her up' is one version of a verse within the rhyme. Does it point to immurement? Some believe that bodies were kept in the base of the bridge, but there has been no evidence at all pointing to this in reality. However, some might say that there is no smoke without fire.

So, back to the present time and just one short week ago, Thursday 8th September 2022, the Prime Minister Liz Truss was given the words 'London Bridge is down'. This was the code name for 'Operation London Bridge', a Metropolitan Police operation regarding the Queen's death. 'London Bridge is down' meant that Queen Elizabeth II had died and the operation regarding her death and funeral arrangements had begun. I wonder why it was called operation London Bridge. Did she have a say in this? London Bridge has stood in one form or another for centuries. A fascinating history. Just like our

Queen. London Bridge being down would have been catastrophic in years gone by. Luckily there were alternatives and replacements built.

As we file past the modern London Bridge I wonder if all those queuing realise that they are walking past an invisible bridge that once stood and housed so many medieval Londoners. I cannot see a plaque or anything that says 'Here once stood the entrance to the medieval London Bridge'. Maybe I missed it.

I look into the river Thames and wonder what we would find if the river was drained. I can only imagine what mysteries might lay beneath this murky water.

As we walk on I'm very pleased to see a sign for The London Bridge Experience. An interactive, immersive experience bringing the history of London Bridge to life through Roman times right up to the Great Fire of London. Thank goodness the history of London Bridge is being kept alive. Again I wonder why living so close, I have never visited. I must be a tourist in my own city more in the future. It would just be rude not to be.

Chapter 7
Mud and Memories

Leaving behind London Bridge we edge slowly forwards, not quite as much of a spring in our step as when in Southwark Park. Time is ticking and tiredness is setting in. My coronation chicken sandwich has long since disappeared into the pit of my stomach and I carefully unwrap the Starbursts one by one in my pocket before popping into my mouth. Yes I'm one of those people. Those that prefer to sneakily eat their sweets than share. Good old Janet is a sharer. Wagon Wheels and pastries. You name it she has it and shares it. A better person than me. My Red Hot Monster Munch are still safely in my bag uneaten. I'll look forward to those later.

Black bollards line the street and tired feet find their owners propped up on the bollards. They make for a good resting spot. It is a shame that they are slightly too tall to perch on but useful nevertheless to rest the rucksack and take a moment. I've heard stories that when some such bollards were once dug up, a whole cannon lay beneath the pavement. It turns out that they were reused for the streets of London following the Battle of Trafalgar in 1805. Many have now been replaced and multiple replicas appear all over the London Boroughs, with the design inspired by the original cannons. If you want to see an original cannon from the battle disguised as a street bollard, one is still in place between Southwark Bridge and Shakespeare's Globe. 250.000 queued past it, mostly unaware of the history lying beneath their feet.

The cannons aren't the only piece of war history reused in London. Stretchers were made in abundance in WW2. Steel poles and wire mesh were used as they were easier to clean following a medical emergency than the traditional fabric. Following the war the stretchers were repurposed into railings. Again, a quick google search will point you in the direction of finding some still in place today. If only metal could talk. What a story these 'bollards' and 'railings' could tell us.

As I look around, most people in the queue are now dressed for the evening weather in coats and hats to keep warm. The sun has set and although now dark, there is light all around from the hustle and bustle on the Thames to the socialites in the bars and restaurants.

The next hour of the walk takes us past multiple eateries and drinking houses. We all look longingly in the windows as we pass. I wonder what the people inside think of us all. Perhaps they think we are crazy but I'm not as worried about what people think as when I was first on the train. Safety in numbers. I'm surrounded by thousands of like-minded people now. We are in this together. What could possibly go wrong?

My phone continues to beep.

"Where are you now?" "Are you ok?" I think everyone is surprised that I decided to queue by myself in London. Of course I have Janet so I'm not really alone but we were strangers at the start of this walk so none of my friends or family have actually met her. There were lots of reports of people making friends for life in the queue. It wasn't like that for me. I guess, as I had never met Janet before, I did make a friend for life, but does it count when it is family? I find it hard enough to make time for the friends and family that I have. Although I must say that the company of the aunt and nieces and David Q and Laura Q was comforting and nice. A bunch of people easy to talk to.

I was very interested in the sightseeing and reading about everything I was passing. Of course this led to dire battery issues. Luckily one of the nieces offered me her portable charger which helped keep me topped up with battery power. I thought that was very kind as who knows if she might need it for herself later. I spent more time researching what I was seeing than talking to those around me. I wanted to enjoy the moment, be part of the history and be mindful of everything as I queued.

Passing cobbled streets and bollards, we edge alongside a pub called 'The Mudlark'. Cobbled streets sound lovely. They are if you don't have plantar fasciitis and haven't been queueing for six hours. Otherwise they are quite unwelcome. We were now at the halfway mark although only hindsight tells me this. I was still convinced we only had a couple more hours to go.

As we wander past the young people, drinking pints and having a merry time in the Mudlark, I ponder on the name. Unusual for a pub. My precious phone battery is needed again for a quick search about the history of the pub. The website for the pub states,

"We often get asked about our unusual name. It comes from the 18th century practice of scavenging the muddy Thames riverbanks for coal, bits of iron and any other valuables that might have fallen off passing ships. The people who took part in this practice, often children, were known as Mudlarks."

It was a known job to be a mudlarker in years gone by. Old nails, coins and items could be sold. It wasn't a big earner. In fact, the poorest of the poor were mudlarkers in the 19th Century. Described as wearing tatty trousers with their feet bandaged they would scour the riverbed for hours on end, day after day, year after year. Their feet bandaged due to the risk of cuts on rocks and stones. Anything they found they would try and sell in order to buy food for their families.

In recent years it is no longer seen as a viable job but a fashionable hobby. Mudlarkers are found regularly along the mud of the tidal Thames looking for snippets of history. You will see them hard at it if you take time to look as you walk the Thames.

The Thames riverbed is a very long site of archaeological interest. The most common find is clay pipes from the dockworkers. Clay pipes were only used once. Recycling wasn't a thing back then. Therefore, many thousands of clay pipes are to be found along the mud of the river.

Any finds over 300 years old must be reported to the Museum of London. If you fancy a go a permit is needed although they have currently paused the issuing of them due to overload. I must get Paul in on the act with his metal detector if the opportunity arises in the future. I wouldn't mind a go myself. I once found an old button which I believed was from some kind of uniform. I found it in the Trenches of Death in Diksmuide Belgium. It became my lucky button, kept safely in my purse. Until I lost my purse one day.

Continuing on, over the cobbled streets and past the black bollards, we once again come across an opening onto the Thames. People are leaving the queue and heading to read a memorial.

"I'm just going to have a look over there." Janet is fine with me popping in and out, happy to queue and hardly rest herself. She oozes happiness, contentment and joy. I count my blessings to have such wonderful company on this amazing experience. I walk over to the memorial just beyond London Bridge, past the Mudlark pub and opposite Southwark Cathedral. I read the following,

"In loving memory. This plaque is placed here, in memory of eight precious lives lost in the terror attacks on London Bridge and Borough on Saturday 3 June 2017." I take a moment, looking right to London Bridge imagining the horror of that day. I can't imagine. I read their names slowly giving due credit to each one. They will be remembered.

Christine Archibald

Sebastien Belanger

Kirsty Boden

Ignacio Echeverria

James McMullean

Alexandre Pigeard

Xavier Thomas

Sara Zelenak

I continue reading.

"We will never forget you, nor all those injured and affected by those terrible events, and the heroes who came to their rescue. Hatred does not cease by hatred, but by love alone."

It is a stark reminder of the modern world we live in. War and terror are not a thing of the past to read about but here now in our society. I bow my head and say to myself "God Bless you all" and rejoin Janet with a heavier heart. So many lives lost once again along the liquid history of the Thames.

Still shuffling along the cobbles, we come across some wonderful concrete pillars. Bottom height. Square in shape. One after another in a line like dominoes. Perfect to sit on. The queue snakes around these pillars for 15 minutes so once again I ask Janet if she'd like to sit. Once again "I'm fine standing" comes the reply. So, don't mind if I do. A wonderful rest once again.

I soon realise that queuers are taking photos of me on the pillars. That's strange, I think to myself. Maybe they have a meaning or some historical feature. We are in London after all. I look around at the pillars and can't say I notice anything historical about them. I feel I should move out of peoples way so that they can get a good shot and so reluctantly stand once more and rejoin Janet.

I look back at the historical pillars. Now I can see what they were looking at. The sight of Southwark Cathedral is quite amazing just beyond the pillars and I realise that this is the photo opportunity. Southwark Cathedral. The photos being taken have The Shard in the background. Old meeting new. A perfect shot. With me photobombing half of them.

Southwark Cathedral has many interesting historical facts. One of the most unusual that strikes me is that it was born out of a Church called 'St. Mary Overie'. Mary was a local ferryman's daughter. Her father used to ferry people across the Thames before the 10th Century. He decided to fake his own death so his servants would fast out of respect. This would save some money. However, they rejoiced and feasted instead! When he jumped out of bed alive he was struck dead by one of the servants for having told a lie. Mary sent for her lover who in haste to get to Mary's inheritance fell off his horse and broke his neck. Punishment for greed or just one of those things? Mary then devoted her inheritance to fund a convent, which eventually became Southwark Cathedral.

The Cathedral has been a place of Christian worship for over 1,000 years, although only a Cathedral since the early 20th Century. As with the medieval stone London Bridge, Southwark Cathedral has also faced fires and rebuilds over the centuries. It has also changed denominations from Catholic to Church of England.

The Cathedral holds numerous graves of people associated with the holy place over the years. Shakespeare's brother was buried within the cathedral upon Shakespeare's request. I find myself considering Shakespeare as a real living person for the first time. He has always just been a name on a book to me. I would like to find out more about his life. I studied the Merchant of Venice at school but can't remember much about it. I do remember the words 'Et tu Brute' and 'Beware the Ides of March'. The Ides of March are the middle of March so I guess the warning is to beware the 15th and 16th March. Funny that. I got married on the 16th March. Also, the two quotes I remember have nothing to do with the Merchant of Venice but Julius Caesar. My learning has got muddled somewhere over the years.

Visiting cathedrals and places of worship has always been an interest of mine. When I went to Stockholm for the Eurovision Song Contest in the year 2000, I found myself wandering around a mosque, church and synagogue. When I used to visit France regularly, I enjoyed visiting the smallest Church I've ever seen in a place called Ulcot. A small hamlet in the Deux-Sevres region. I find it moving and spiritual to sit in a place of worship. I feel really at peace. Protected somehow. Of course, the gravestones surrounding the place of worship also get a good visit out of me too. Today, there's no time to pop into the cathedral whilst in the queue and the gates look shut anyway so no missed opportunity this evening.

My phone rings.

"Hi Mum when will you be home?"

"Hi Emily, I'm not sure. A few more hours. You'll be in bed but I'll come in to see you."

"Okay bye."

The phone goes down as I begin to talk some more. Emily likes to know when I'll be home. She's less interested in the detail and once she's had her say and found out what she needs, that's the call over. I haven't spoken to Amy in a while, so I keep my phone out and call her.

"Are you nearly there yet? Where are you? Have you had dinner?"

Amy likes to know the detail.

I indulge myself and her with the story so far in a nutshell so as to conserve my battery and then hang up. I wish they were with me, seeing what I could see and experiencing what I was experiencing. Emily was too young, aged ten, and Amy, aged sixteen, had been content enough with seeing the flowers at Buckingham Palace.

I think of others that would have liked to be with me. My mum and dad and my mother-in-law Sue. They would have thoroughly enjoyed the slow walk and historical feeling of the moment. I look forward to telling them all about it. Hopefully one day they can all 'walk the queue' with me and I can point things out to them along the way.

As I went to put my phone away, I thought I'd have a quick glance at the news. 'Man detained by police after he 'ran up to Queen's coffin' in Westminster Hall'. Oh no. This isn't good news. Why on earth would someone do this to someone's coffin? Queen or not. Even more reason not to do so when there are armed police and guards everywhere. I wonder what his motivation and reasons were? It hits me again that this is a huge police operation. Any signs of trouble in Westminster Hall and I'd lie flat on the floor. I had it planned. I wonder if I had have been in there when this had happened if I would have flung myself dramatically on the floor in a panic? I'm pleased that I wasn't there. Anything untoward, outside the boundary of rules, makes me nervous. I decide to turn off my phone, save my battery and save myself any unnecessary panics.

The queue is on the move. We walk past an interesting looking building called Minerva House and cast a final glance at Southwark Cathedral before turning the corner and coming face to face with a group of scouts playing pirates on a replica of a 16th Century Galleon.

Chapter 8
Old London Town

A magnificent black boat that looks like it has come straight out of a pirate movie is in front of us. Covered in yellow and red stripes, with scouts chanting, cheering and looking like they are about to go into battle. When I was 12 I don't remember having such a good roleplay prop. It was more like old bedsheets hung over the washing line for a makeshift tent creating hours of fun. I remember playing in the garden on long summer days and long summer evenings. Time seems to speed up as you get older. Not in this queue though. The longest queue in history. Mentally the time is fine, physically it's a bit harder. The evening air is chilly. Jumpers, coats and woolly hats are still evident on many. As we are all hustled together, constantly moving there's not time for feet to get cold which probably helps.

The queue snakes around the left of the boat and all heads are turned towards it, enthralled and captured by the scout's re-enactment. One of them is shouting instructions and they are all chanting back in response. It could almost be a play with us as the audience. Us queuers are all the same. Nosey and interested. A detailed information board satisfies our curiosity and fills in our knowledge gaps on this magnificent boat:

"In 1577, The Golden Hinde set sail from Plymouth, captained by Francis Drake, her mission was to sail to the Pacific, explore new territories and raid Spanish colonies and shipping. Nearly three years later, The Golden Hinde arrived back in England laden with valuable cargo having cemented her place in history as the first English ship to circumnavigate the world. Drake was knighted for his successes and continued to play a key role in English maritime history. The Golden Hinde herself was berthed in a dry dock in Deptford as a museum ship, where she was open for public exhibition. Sadly, almost nothing now remains of the original ship, which had succumbed to rot by the mid-1600's.

The full-scale reconstruction of the Golden Hinde was launched in April 1973. Commissioned by Golden Hinde Ltd of San Francisco, she was designed by Californian naval architect Loring Christian Norgaard after years of meticulous research. Built using tradition techniques at J. Hinks and Sons Shipyard in Appledore, Devon, she represents a milestone in the history of naval architecture.

On the 1st of October, 1974, the reconstructed Golden Hinde began her first adventure. Since then, she has circumnavigated the globe, completed multiple Atlantic crossings and worked as a museum around the world, sailing over 100,000 miles. Since being invited to St. Mary Overie Dock in 1996, The Golden Hinde has served as a museum with a range of programmes, events and performances designed to breathe life into history."

I'm left slightly disappointed it isn't the real thing and is instead an almost 50 year old replica. I imagine my disappointment stems from being spoilt by the historical sights in London up to this point. Still, it's pleasing to see history being kept alive with the reconstructed Golden Hinde. The Scouts are certainly not disappointed. They might as well be in battle on the real thing for all the shouts and squeals of delight that I can hear. My brother-in-law Vinal is a Scout leader. I must mention to him that this could be his Friday night if he wanted it to be.

Merry singing and jovial chatter sound out the Scouts. We are like meerkats peering from one sight to the next.

The Old Thameside Inn. Another pub following the Mudlark and the Angel. This queue could well be a pub crawl. Now a pub crawl is something I haven't been on since my university days. This Southbank is an ideal place for one. Some queuers rush to the bar to buy drinks again and then run along the side of the queue trying to find their place. For most of us though it's about keeping warm and moving now. As we look at the Friday night drinkers, they too look at us. I'm not sure who is in the zoo here, us or them.

The Old Thameside Inn is a pretty sight. Festoon lights with the backdrop of the Thames next to the Golden Hinde, with makeshift tables made of barrels to fit the scene. It makes for a good atmosphere for a night out alongside the Golden Hinde. No wonder it is busy and full of people. Again, we are entertained by the general London public, but our mission is strictly full steam ahead. No pun intended.

My thoughts turn once again to why we are here queueing for hours. The death of Her Majesty Queen Elizabeth II. I'm beginning to think maybe I am quite the royalist after all. Why else would I be doing this? We see on our phones that members of the Royal Family, the grandchildren, have recently stood guard at the Queen's coffin. Prince William, Prince Harry standing at the head and foot of the coffin as requested by King Charles III. Joined by their cousins Princess Beatrice, Princess Eugenie, Zara Tindell, Peter Philips, Lady Louise and Viscount Severn. Now that would be something to see. If only that took place as it was our turn to enter Westminster Hall. No-one could possibly time their queue place correctly to ensure such a thing. Just luck of the draw.

Whenever I see someone famous, I'm always surprised by how small and human they seem. On the TV their characters make them seem different, untouchable somehow. It was a similar experience when I met Princess Anne. We had a royal visit to the school I worked in back in 2002. I had a small class of children with additional needs and we awaited her arrival wondering what we should be doing as she enters the classroom. I decided to pick up a guitar and play it and sing a song. The students were having great fun. They didn't notice that I couldn't play and I was just strumming along.

Along came Princess Anne in her long coat and knee high boots, hair swooped up into a twist. She had a little chat with both myself and the students and left to move on to the next classroom. I wish I could remember some more about it but I can't. The students were happy and excited although they didn't fully understand the momentous occasion for our school. The day Santa Claus arrived by helicopter to the school field was probably the most memorable occasion for many of them, and me, at the time.

I never saw the Queen but still feel like she was part of my life. Always there. Stable and consistent. As I got older I enjoyed the Queen's Speech at Christmas more and more. The speech during covid really touched me as I'm sure it did many people. The NHS choir, images from the pandemic and the words 'We'll meet again'. Then the images of her sitting alone at Prince Philips funeral. What a role model to us all. No wonder people were angry when some others didn't keep the rules.

I've recently read that the Royal Family costs each person in the UK £1.50 a year. For the amount of work they do, non-political charitable advocating and bringing the country together, it's the best £1.50 we could possibly spend. Let alone the tourism, the economy, sporting events and the work bringing faiths together.

Sometimes I worry about the future of the monarchy, but thankfully they do seem to ride out every storm in their path. King Charles III and Prince William have proven to be dedicated and I look forward to hopefully seeing Prince William have his turn in the future also. King Charles III has been famous for saying in the past that he will not only be 'Defender of the faith' but also 'Defender of faith'. This is a great move towards community solidarity. I always seem to mention this in my R.E. lessons.

We leave the Scouts to their cheers and dramatic action poses and the merry drinkers getting more and more merry by the minute and continue on our mission.

The queue condenses the closer we get to Westminster Hall and there is slightly more stoppage time than usual. The nieces behind are enjoying their little stools they are managing to sit on every half hour or so for a minute or two and ask if I would like to sit. I say "no thank you" although I would actually like to sit. The getting up again is hard though so it seems easier on the feet to just keep going.

All of a sudden I hear some arguing from behind us. A slightly louder group than ourselves are telling someone not to push in. I don't like the confrontation, so I stay out of it although the queue pusher is almost next to me. He promises he has been queuing all along.

However, everyone knows who is in front and behind so I wonder how this can be true.

Then I realise.

As the queue moves and stops, moves and stops, it appears he has just been moving and so 'walking the queue' at a normal pace on the periphery of everyone. Until he passes the loud crowd of course who catch him out and put him in his place. He eventually retreats a few people behind them and doesn't try any more shenanigans.

As we turn the corner from the Old Thameside Inn and the Golden Hinde, another wow sight beholds us. A magnificent, ruined wall, backed by modern wharf conversions. Old and new once again side by side emphasising the age and historicalness of the wall. It looks like a church wall with an intricate concrete rose window. It is the ruins of Winchester Palace, sometimes called Winchester House.

Building began in 1107 by the then Bishop of Winchester, William Gifford. His successor, Henri de Blois, King Henry I's nephew, extended and completed the palace in 1144. The palace was home to bishops staying in London. They had gardens and tennis courts alongside the more obvious features such as the Great Hall. It was in this hall that James I of Scotland held his wedding feast. Royal visitors were regular and again we are reminded of the monarchy's long history in London. It is reported that Henry VIII met his fifth wife Catherine Howard at Winchester Palace. He was also known to frequent it for its 'Winchester Geese' also known as working women.

In the 17th Century the palace was repurposed as tenements and warehouses. Ruins were then discovered in the 19th Century and are preserved for us to ponder on today.

One key feature of Winchester Palace was its very own prison. From as early as the 9th Century, the Church had cells for penance. It was commonplace in medieval times for bishops to have cells. Ecclesiastical prisons as they were called.

The Bishop of Winchester residing at the Palace licensed 22 brothels along the riverside. That's right. The Bishop regulated the brothels. Many crimes in relation to this were punishable by prison. For this reason, Winchester Palace housed the first women's prison in the U.K. alongside the men's.

The prison became known as 'The Clink' and the surrounding area 'The Clink Liberty'.

Royal connections are varied and many. Edward VII and Mary I frequented the Clink Liberty for council meetings and Henry VII left two thousand pounds in his will for the prisoners in the Clink. He must have felt some affiliation or sorrow for the prisoners. I can only imagine the conditions.

As we edge past the ruins of Winchester Palace, tourist signs appear 'Free photo behind bars', 'England's oldest prison', 'Prisoners this way', 'Torture your friends', (no thank you). Finally, we see what the attraction is, 'The Clink, 1144-1780, most notorious medieval prison, voted by the people'.

It's still here. The Clink. As I look above the sign I see a skeleton hanging.

Life as a prisoner in medieval times was no fun at all. In the late 12th Century The Clink legalised physical torment for the prisoners. Whipping and stoning were common practice. The dungeons had chains, manacles and fetters to hold prisoners in great discomfort. Of course, this depended on how noble you were. The very rich had more comfortable accommodation on the Knights side. The Masters side was saved for the affluent and the Hole was saved for the very poor.

The worst thing I read about the Hole was prisoners standing naked in water until their feet rotted. The reason they were naked is that they sold their clothes for more food. They would beg at the gratings at street level. I imagine Oliver Twist style escapades at street level through the grate.

Hunger, thirst and cold were everyday problems as well as the risk of murder. Prostitution also still took place within the prison walls and disease was rife.

In 1450 an uprising saw the Clink burnt down and prisoners released. The 16th Century saw mostly heretics imprisoned with the 17th Century seeing mostly debtors. Blimey we could all have ended up in the Clink for not paying a credit card or refusing to believe in God. The 17th Century also saw prisoners dying like flies from the plague. I wonder if the guy selling apples on London Bridge ended up dying from the plague in the Clink prison? It's probably very likely.

After centuries of use the Clink began to decay beyond repair and a new prison was eventually rented on another sight.

As we pass the entrance with the queuers heads peering down the steps into the entrance a sign reads 'You are now entering the original site of the Clink the prison that gave its name to all others'. It looks like a dungeon, dark, gloomy and scary. I'm not sure I would fancy an hour tour let alone a prison sentence there 700 years ago.

Then again, I'm now intrigued and can imagine being back here visiting before long. The most I know about prisons is the few mentions of Holloway that my Dad mentioned over the years. I'm not sure of the conditions there but it must have been better than the original Clink.

We enter a dark, old tunnel leading away from the Clink. An old looking winch, no longer in use is fitted to the side of the tunnel. I wonder what it was used for. It must have been the movement of goods as we have been surrounded by wharfs.

I'm lost in my thoughts again. Chatter continues around me as we pass a Premier Inn. If only I'd have had the foresight to book a room so no concerns over getting home. Never mind, maybe it can be a place to return to in order to re-walk the queue one day. Re-walk the queue? I haven't even finished queuing and yet I'm planning to return. This is what makes the queue feel like a pilgrimage. A special moment in time that affects you spiritually. It is unexpected, welcoming and surprising all at once. I turn to Janet and say,

"I think I'll come back and 'walk the queue.'"

"Count me in" she replies.

Chapter 9
Bankside

The Queen's Queue could almost be renamed the Bankside pub crawl. What an array of watering holes. From old inns to modern bars. They line the Thames today just as they have done for centuries. Some queuers, although few now, are making the most of the opportunity to get a cold drink or use the facilities. Others are drowning in the atmosphere as they pass making mental notes to return and try out the various outlets.

It's dark. There is a late summer chill in the air and coats and hats are getting their full use as we pass more and more Friday night revellers enjoying a beverage or two in one of the liquid establishments.

Aptly named, after passing the wharfs and the Clink, the Anchor pub has a prominent corner position with a Thameside view. With it's twinkly lights and an outside bar for convenience, it's easy to see why it is bustling with London's social scene. Across the Thames we can see St. Paul's Cathedral rising prominently amongst the landscape of the North Bank. The most picturesque setting for a Friday night social. Only there are thousands of people queuing alongside them this evening, perhaps taking from the atmosphere or maybe enhancing it? Either way, the queuers think the Anchor is quite a majestic sight.

The Anchor pub has had its fair share of history and is not only known for being along the route of the Queen's Queue, but it is also known for being the place where Samuel Pepys sat and watched London burn in 1666. Thankfully after some days of burning the fire didn't cross London Bridge. The reason being that there was a significant gap where homes were destroyed due to another earlier fire a few years earlier. This gap enabled the fire to peter out as it created a 'fire break'.

Another fire in 1676 in Borough High Street destroyed 500 buildings. Under Charles II direction, buildings in the fire's path were destroyed in order to stop the fire from spreading. Lessons had been learnt from the great fire and the knocking down of buildings to create 'fire breaks' were the saving grace.

If you want to know more about life in medieval London, the diary of Samuel Pepys, a naval administrator and Member of Parliament is a must read. Written between 1660 and 1669 it details not only the private life of Pepys but also acts as a memoir of the 17th century.

I spy a detailed information board about the Anchor pub and wander over to read. One of the best things about this queue is that you don't lose your place. Although we mostly shuffle along together, there are comings and goings all the time as people pop into a shop or to the toilet or to read a local sign.

I take time to read the sign which reads:

"The brewery site, upon which this present building stands, has a rich and varied past. Throughout history 'The Anchor' has been used as a tavern, a brothel, a chapel, a brewery, ships chandlers and has entertained a wealth of notable patrons.

The first official record of 'The Anchor' was not made until 1822. However, other records state that, as well as being the site of a roman grave, the locality was used for plague pits during 1603 and old maps show bear and bull baiting pits within the site. It was most likely that one early owner of the brewery, Josiah Childs (1665), gave 'The Anchor' it's current name. Childs was closely involved with the Royal Navy to whom he supplied 'masts, spars and bowsprits as well as stores and small beer'. At one time the locals referred to this pub as 'Thrales of deadman's place' - 'Thrales' being the name of the brewery who owned the pub at the time.

Perhaps the most famous local landmark was the original Globe Theatre, which stood from 1598-1613. Performed here were Shakespearian classics such as 'Romeo and Juliet' and 'As you like it'. Many other London pubs claim Shakespeare as a patron, although we can be fairly sure he enjoyed an ale or two within these walls. The modern 'Shakespeares Globe' opened in 1997, is a reconstruction of the original theatre, built within metres of the previous building.

Dr Samuel Johnson, another of England's best known literary figures, was a close friend of the Thrale brewery owners and a regular patron at 'The Anchor'. As the single most quoted English writer after Shakespeare, Dr Johnson wrote many essays, poems and books, including his dictionary of the English language. A copy of his dictionary is on display in the pub. Johnson was a member of the literary club, founded by Sir Joshua Reynolds in 1764 which included many influential, cultural figures of the time. In May 1773 a superb meal was enjoyed at 'The Anchor' with these friends and associates including Reynolds (Artist), Oliver Goldsmith (Irish Poet), David

Garrick (Actor and Author of 'Heart of Oak are our Ships') and Edmund Burke (Anglo/Irish Statesman).

It was from the pub that in 1666, famous diarist Samuel Pepys witnessed the awesome destruction of the Great Fire of London. He wrote in his personal diary that he took refuge in 'a little alehouse on Bankside ... and there watched the fire grow'. The Great Fire swept through the central parts of London. Gutting the medieval city and destroying the majority of London's homes. The original pub survived the great fire of 1666. Ironically it burned down sometime later when fire devastated the area, and was rebuilt between 1770-1775 by Win Allen, to become the pub we see today.

The pub contains a room dedicated to the 'Clink Prison' which can be found nearby in the aptly named Clink Street. The Clink, owned by the Bishop of Winchester, was built for the detention of religious non-conformists and was in use from the 12th century until 1780 when it was burned down during the Gordon Riots and was never rebuilt. The Clink Prison was the first prison in which women were regularly confined."

A lot of history for one site. I look across the Thames imagining I'm Samuel Pepys watching the Great Fire of London spreading. I imagine the Anchor filled with merry men and quite possibly 'Winchester Geese' now I know it once served as a brothel. I imagine the plague victims buried underneath. History all around us.

As quite the animal lover since becoming a pet mum to my beloved Buddy, bear baiting sounds cruel and barbaric. It was a vicious sport Londoners used to enjoy for entertainment. Bears were imported from Northern Europe and used alongside bulls and dogs in fights. Londoners paid to enter the arena and money was made through bets. I'm pleased to say that this sport died out in the 17th Century.

What a gift I feel I have been given. Not only to pay my respects to the late Queen Elizabeth II but also to all those whose historical accounts I am discovering as I walk. The plague sufferers, the Clink prisoners, the Winchester geese, Dr. Salter. When does anyone get a chance to actually slow walk for 12 hours taking everything in. What a lesson for us all. We must slow down in life as we just miss so much.

I look around and it turns out the queue has moved quite quickly whilst I had been reading and daydreaming. I quick march to catch up with my people. You can't go wrong, just keep walking and you soon find them.

All huddled together walking along the Thames I find we are quite warm with all the close proximity keeping us cosy. We pass a lifeboats life ring. We have probably passed a number of them but I notice this one particularly as a light from somewhere shines against the red.

Over the years, thousands have lost their lives in the 'liquid history' of the Thames through disasters and otherwise. I look out at the shimmering water and imagine the death and sadness that has been experienced here.

The heads on stakes on London Bridge were eventually thrown into the river. William Wallace and Guy Fawkes' heads are out there somewhere.

As we walk along between Cannon Street railway bridge and head towards Southwark Bridge I am reminded of the Marchioness disaster. A party boat in 1989 that collided with another boat. Sadly, 51 people lost their lives.

The ferrymen who used to ferry people backwards and forwards across the Thames, before the abundance of bridges we see today, also sometimes took life into their own hands. The Thames was a choppy tidal river and not all made their crossings safely.

Every so often the Thames used to freeze over completely. The ferrymen were not happy at this. It meant they would be losing their money ferrying people across. Instead, they used to try and charge people to enter the ice. Some even went as far as to destroy the ice from the shore to a couple of metres out so that then they could charge people to cross the small section of water. Anything to make some money.

Complaints about the ferrymen led to boats being licensed, much like the black taxis of London today. This enabled the public to have greater faith in the ferrymen and the conning of the public became more difficult.

We suddenly hear some music. Shoulders start to wiggle and legs start to tap. It's a busker singing in a small tunnel we are about to pass through. At last some musical entertainment. I've been waiting for this ever since the Southwark Park bandstand. A little music brings a smile to all faces and really helps to keep everyone upbeat.

A family friend once used a busker playing a harp at her wedding. I've always thought what a great way to find talent. Just walk the streets of London.

There's an array of concrete inscriptions behind the busker and to my delight they tell the story of the frost fairs held on the Thames.

"Behold the liquid Thames now frozen or'e

That lately Ship of mighty Burthen bore

The Watermen for want of Rowing Boats

Make ufe of Booths to get their Pence & Groats

Here you may fee Beef Roafted on the Spit,

And for your Money you may tafte a bit

Here you may print your Name, tho cannot write,

Caufe num'd with Cold: Tis done with great Delight"

Frost fairs took place when the Thames froze over. These icy moments on the Thames attracted stall holders and entertainers and soon 'Frost Fairs' were a regular occurrence in medieval times. It has been said that Henry VIII enjoyed sleigh rides on the Thames.

In the 16th Century the Thames froze for ten weeks! Stalls set themselves up on the ice and it became an ice carnival for weeks on end.

The last frost fair was in the early 19th Century. Or was it? I spied a poster on our walk to the Queen. It had an image of a fire eater and said 'Banksides Frost Fair. Art. Food. Merriment. A feast of art, food, drink and events to celebrate Bankside's historic Frost Fairs'. It was to run from the beginning of December to the end of January this year! How lovely that this historic tradition was being kept alive, although I doubt they would pull off freezing the Thames over today. It must be alongside the Thames instead.

As we exit the tunnel and now stand on the other side of Southwark Bridge, I see a bollard that I am certain is not a replica but a real cannon bollard. Why do I think this is a real one? It looks older than the rest and it has an actual hole in the top. Filled with cigarette butts maybe, but it's definitely different from the other shiny black bollards seen thus far. It sits right by the steps leading up to Southwark Bridge on the west side of the South Bank if ever you find yourself 'walking the queue'.

Southwark Bridge was built to ease the London traffic and opened in 1819. 102 years later, the bridge was replaced due to its steep gradient. It is still one of the least popular bridges today for traffic. The areas it serves are less popular that others along the river.

As I look over the river wall it looks like a mudlarkers dream with old wooden posts and piers and stones. History to my right, yet on my left modern restaurants a plenty. No mudlarkers are out now as it is late and dark but come the morning they will be back. Although mudlarking licenses are currently on hold, you can book a mudlarking experience if you want to give it a try.

Between two restaurants there is a small road called 'Bear Gardens'. It sounds as though it houses some trendy outlets but alas it does not. It is down this road that the last Bear Baiting pit stood. A popular sport for centuries that saw bears, bulls and dogs fighting each other for their lives. Some bear baiting pits became theatres on some days of the week and bear pits other days of the week. No wonder the theatrical bankside was met with suspicion as an entertainment alongside bear baiting and brothels. I wonder if there are bear bones waiting for an archaeologist to find one day. There surely must be numerous dog bones. The brutality of what went on in this road beggars belief.

You don't even need to wander into the road to see something else significant on the wall on the side of the Greek restaurant in Bear Gardens.

It is a medieval ferryman's seat.

These seats used to be all along the river. A slab of stone sticking out as a seat along with steps down into the boats. The ferryman's seat is a surviving seat displayed for all interested in the historic bankside to see. If only the seat, or more like slab of stone, could speak. What stories might it tell? Who did this ferryman seat belong to? Who did he take across the river each day? Did he cheat his customers? What did he do during the frost fairs? Did anyone die under his watch? What were his family like?

I look around in the queue and wonder if people back then were just like us queuers. Keen to fit in, obey the law, pay respects and find joy in company. I wonder if they queued to pay their respects to their reigning King or Queen when they died. I cannot imagine many in this queue enjoying bear baiting but sports yes. Maybe those that enjoyed it back then were just a victim of their times, as we are a victim of our times. For example, spending too much time procrastinating online.

I then start to wonder if some people in the queue are ghosts, just like on the underground. I point out a few to myself that look like they might be but decide to shake myself back into the living. I'm tired, my mind is wandering more and it is probably time for some more food. I haven't managed the Red Hot Monster Munch yet. I'm not sure why as they usually wouldn't last this long. I still don't fancy them so I go for the Wagon Wheel Janet kindly gave me earlier.

Before I can start to consider where the name Wagon Wheel came from, my mind is saved by some more notes to read. 'Building Bankside'.

A construction site has ensured its boards tell the story of where we stand in the queue. Once, where we stand would have been under water as the Thames was much wider years ago. With no embankments in the medieval centuries the Thames spread much further inland. It also seems the history here goes well beyond the medieval era with bronze age farming and settlements having been found in some areas near London Bridge and Southwark Cathedral.

We carry on along the Thames, past Bankside pier and watch the Uber boats fill up and move up and down the river. I wonder who gets an Uber boat to work? How fashionable and modern. It even has a tube style map with various lines running and overall there are twenty Thames clippers boats in service today.

With all this modernness you would think queues might have changed a bit over the years. Perhaps bring in walking escalators like at airports or something similar. There must be something, we just haven't thought of it yet. I glance at my phone and reply to yet more messages. My sister Emma asking how it's going. Paul asking where I am now.

I take the opportunity to have a quick glance at the queue app. It says 14 hours queue time with the start still in Southwark Park. So many thousands of people still joining the queue. I will let you into a secret here. Once I was home and my feet had rested, I felt like doing it all again the Saturday night with Paul, Amy and Emily. I wanted them to experience what I had experienced. Words could not do it justice.

I take out my Queen Elizabeth biography for children and begin to flick through the chapters looking at the names. I am determined to know more about the woman I am going to pay respects to. I know she was never born to be Queen and took on the role after her father died and after he had taken the throne from his brother who abdicated. I know that she was in Africa when she found out she was Queen. Also that she was a great servant to this country and was well loved and respected. She loved her corgis and horses and her children and her grandchildren. I know about her homes and charitable work. What else can I find out before this queue ends?

Chapter 10
Her Majesty Queen Elizabeth II

I had first better explain why I am reading a children's biography. It's quite simple really. I find when I am looking for information, children's books are the first go to. When studying St. Paul at university, I bought a detailed theological book entitled 'Pauline Theology'. I also bought three children's books telling the story of St. Paul. You cannot begin to understand the depth and detail without first knowing the basics. Children's books are fabulous for easy reads and quick information. I studied Jane Eyre at school. I read the easy version and watched the film. Ok I may have missed some important language points but I wasn't studying for a degree and it helped me to understand.

When I was pregnant with Amy I had a book called K.I.S.S. Pregnancy which meant Keep It Simple Series. It is the best way to learn. I also had a K.I.S.S. Gardening book. From that I designed a lovely garden with pots and herbs in my first ever mortgaged house in Scotland.

Needless to say that's where my gardening skills began and ended. My garden is a victim of the modern day busy life and is mostly neglected. Luckily it's small.

Back to the Queen and my child friendly book, it was time to find out more. As I had just the hours in the queue to read about the Queen, I had grabbed a book that was on the side in the kitchen. I had bought it for my daughter a few days earlier and luckily managed to squeeze it into my 'queue bag'.

So Queen Elizabeth II. Who were you? Do we already know everything? I probably do but I need a reminder and what better place than whilst I queue.

I tell Janet I'm just going to flick through my book. Even though it's now dark there is a glow of city life and I am able to read quickly and easily by the street lamps and the London nightlife lights.

Born Elizabeth Alexandra Mary Windsor on 21st April 1926, she was the first child of Elizabeth and Albert. Albert was an important man. He was the King's son, so Elizabeth was born into a wealthy and well known family. Albert's brother David was one day to become King. This was Elizabeth's uncle.

Elizabeth grew up in a terraced house in London. 145 Piccadilly. She had a happy childhood looked after by a nanny and loved by her parents. She struggled to pronounce her own name and called herself 'Lillibet'. This is her nickname that we the public have all come to know over the past few years. Her recent great granddaughter being named after her.

Elizabeth was a happy child. She loved rocking horses and owned many of them. Aged only four years old, her grandfather King George V bought her a real pony that she named 'Peggy' and so began her love affair with horses.

There are varying accounts as to how old Elizabeth was when she received her first corgi, whom she named 'Dookie'. Regardless of when the first one came into her life, Corgis surrounded the Queen throughout her reign.

Elizabeth was an intelligent young girl and worked hard at home with her governess 'Crawfie'. People that were wealthy like her didn't get sent to school, instead she had a home education.

(I hope you are liking the straightforward factual info as much as I liked reading it)

Elizabeth was ten years old when her life changed dramatically. Her Uncle David abdicated from the throne in order to marry a divorced woman. This meant that Elizabeth's father became King. She had to leave her home and move into Buckingham Palace. As she was now first in line to become Queen her lessons changed and she had to learn all about the British Empire and the monarchy and countries around the world.

Aged just 13, Elizabeth met her future husband, a sea cadet named Philip, when her family visited the Royal Naval College at Dartmouth. Too young to be thinking of a love affair, their romance blossomed some years later.

During the war Elizabeth gave a speech to all the children to help them feel reassured. She said "Thousands of you in this country have had to leave your homes and be separated from your fathers and mothers. My sister Margaret Rose and I feel so much for you as we know from experience what it means to be away from those we love most of all". Indeed, the sisters did know the suffering children were facing as they too were sent away to protect them from London bombings themselves and were taken to reside at Windsor Castle.

The speech was to be the first of many. The Queen's speech has been a prominent fixture on Christmas Day throughout her reign. There is even a film named 'The Queen's Speech'. It is an iconic address to the nation. The speech includes the ups and downs of the previous year and reassurances of good things to come. Always uplifting, poignant and relevant, the Queen's speech sought to unite the nation and generally succeeded in doing so.

Following Elizabeth's first speech the war progressed, as did Elizabeth in age. She became a member of the Auxiliaries and trained as a mechanic in order to 'do her bit' for the war effort. The Royal Family are never likely to shy away from working for their country when needed. They lead by example and keep the great British spirit alive.

Following the victorious celebrations of the ending of the Second World War Elizabeth agreed to marry Prince Philip. The wedding took place in 1947 and was a joyous occasion.

In 1948 their first baby boy was born. Charles Philip Arthur George. 1950 saw the arrival of Anne Elizabeth Alice Louise. Life was filled with happiness whilst the family lived in Malta where Prince Philip was stationed with the Royal Navy but alas, it was short lived as Elizabeth soon had to take up royal duties on behalf of her ailing father back in the U.K.

Tours, speeches and meetings filled their lives until one day, when Elizabeth was just 26 years old, her father died and she became Queen. She was in Kenya at the time and had to return before her tour had even begun. Her new title would be 'Queen Elizabeth II, by the Grace of God Queen of this Realm and of Her other Realms and Territories, Head of the Commonwealth, Defender of the Faith'. Quite a responsibility for one so young.

Queen Elizabeth II's Coronation took place on a rainy day in June 1953 to cries of 'God save the Queen'. By this time Queen Elizabeth II had taken on the role like a duck to water. Holding weekly audiences with the Prime minister and dealing with correspondence via the red box were just some of her day to day and week to week duties.

In 1960 the family welcomed a second son, Andrew Albert Christian Edward. Four years later the family was complete with the arrival of Edward Antony Richard Louis.

In 1967, the Queen named a Cunard cruise liner, replacing the old Queen Elizabeth. She launched the ship by saying "I name this ship

Queen Elizabeth the Second". It has now been out of service since 2008 and resides in Dubai as a floating hotel. Talking of ships, the Royal Family also owned a much loved yacht called 'Britannia'. Holidays were taken on the yacht by all members of the Royal Family and it became a home from home.

The QE2 cruise liner name took off. Not everything named by the Queen has had the same fortune. The Dartford Bridge, as we mostly call it, is named the Queen Elizabeth II Bridge, yet 'Dartford Bridge' is how locals refer to it. Perhaps in the future it might become more well known as the QE2 bridge?

Despite Queen Elizabeth II's success in fulfilling her duty, there were some difficult moments to endure also. In 1981, she survived what at first appeared to be an attempted assassination when riding her horse during the Trooping of the Colour. It turned out the gun fired was without bullets.

1992 was a most difficult year for the Queen. Prince Charles, Princess Anne and Prince Andrew's marriages all broke down. As the Royal Family should be setting an example and as herself, Head of the

Church of England, the Queen wasn't happy with the reputation of her family at this time.

As if that wasn't enough there was also a fire at Windsor Castle, destroying large parts of the castle. The Queen herself named the year 'annus horribilus'.

Something good that came from the fire was Buckingham Palace began opening it's doors to the public. This helped with the funding for the repairs. It remains open to this day in the summer months and on other selected dates. I am sure that this not only helps with the finances but also with the public and crown relations. The more accessible the monarchy, the longer it can survive.

Other difficult moments in her reign included the Aberfan disaster of 1966 which saw 144 people killed when a local colliery waste tip slid on top of a school and village in Wales. Locals were angry that the Queen did not visit to pay her respects until eight days after the disaster. However, preparing for a royal visit takes time and spontaneity isn't easy.

The Queen also had some difficult decisions to make regarding her sister. She wanted her sister Princess Margaret to be happy and marry the man she loved despite him being a divorced man. Yet as Queen she could not allow Princess Margaret to remain in line to the throne and marry the man she loved as well. It was not appropriate to marry a divorcee. Princess Margaret chose the Royal Family line and ended her love affair. This is in contrast to their Uncle David who had chosen to give up his title and marry his divorced love.

The Queen was also under the spotlight when Princess Diana was killed in a car crash in Paris. The divorced wife of her son Prince Charles. Controversy abounded the divorce and relationships were strained. Queen Elizabeth II didn't immediately return to Buckingham Palace, instead opting to stay with her grandchildren in Scotland and comfort them. Damned if you do, damned if you don't springs to mind.

More sadness followed eight years later. The Queen was particularly close to both her sister Margaret and her mother and was devastated when they died within six weeks of each other in 2002.

Further difficulties came in 2019 with scandal surrounding her son Prince Andrew, leading him to be stripped of his royal titles and stopping work as a royal.

Her grandson Prince Harry then chose to step back as a working royal in 2020. More negative media ensued with the Queen showing her constant dignity throughout.

2021 saw the death of her husband Prince Philip aged 99. He was only two months away from receiving a telegram from the Queen for his 100th birthday. Due to covid restrictions, Queen Elizabeth II sat by herself in St. George's Chapel, strictly adhering to covid guidelines. It was a sad sight to see. The Queen herself, alone, at her husband's funeral.

Lasting memories of the Queen include her extra address to the nation during covid when she ended with 'We'll meet again' followed by images of the pandemic and emergency services helping all those affected. Uniting the nation in the way she knows best, the Queen sought to comfort, reassure and give hope and that's exactly what she did.

Any feminism within the Queen's views were always traditional and respectful. In 1979, Britain welcomed its first female prime minister. A Queen and a female prime minister! One would hope for intimate tea parties and girly chats but it wasn't quite how things turned out. It is widely believed that the relationship was 'icy'.

In 2013, the Queen agreed to a new law whereby any descendent of the monarchy can become next in line, whether male or female. Up until this point, a brother, no matter the age, would always supersede his sister. This was a very important change. Gender equality laws are infiltrating our society for the better, yet there is still a lack of women in leadership. If a woman cannot become Queen simply because she has a brother, it is a message to all that men lead better. This new law of 2013 is a clear message that the sexes are equal in leadership and in monarchy. Well done Queen Elizabeth II.

I cannot dedicate a chapter to some basic information about the Queen's reign without mentioning her fashion. One of her dresses was loaned to Princess Beatrice as her wedding gown. I remember thinking it was one of the loveliest wedding dresses I have ever seen. Vintage and classic yet different.

What I remember most about the Queen's wardrobe is either her later years with her bright coloured dresses and coats with hat and bag or her Barbour wax jackets. Her earlier style I don't remember as she was over 70 for most of my adult life.

Over the course of Queen Elizabeth II's reign she became patron of over 600 charities. These included various genres from agriculture to the arts to businesses to education to faith to healthcare to science and sport. In 2016 she held the Patron's lunch to honour her 90th birthday. This consisted of a street party on the Mall with 10,000 guests invited representing various charities where the Queen was a patron.

Queen Elizabeth enjoyed celebrating with the public. For her 80th birthday, she invited 99 people from around the world to celebrate over lunch with her. Those people that were invited also shared her birthday and turned 80 on the same day. It sounds like a good idea to me. I'd quite enjoy having a party with 99 others born on the same day as me. Kindred spirits aligned by the stars, or something like that.

Queen Elizabeth II was the longest reigning monarch in the history of this country. Her reign lasted over 70 years. One speech that sums up her service was actually delivered before she became Queen. It shows her dedication to the life ahead of her. We can now say with certainty that she kept her promise.

"I declare before you all that my whole life whether it be long or short, shall be devoted to your service and the service of our great imperial family to which we all belong" (1947)

Chapter 11
This is St. Bartholomew's Fair

As the crowds took their seats, I took a step up and stood behind the curtain. As the welcome began, I shuffled in my place. I was nervous and excited all at once. An introduction ensued, applause and then hush.

The curtains began to move. Dressed in old jeans and an untucked shirt I made my way into the bright lights and took centre stage.

Market stall holders and crowds appeared from the wings. I took a further step forwards. This was my moment. My one line of the whole show. The opening line. My teacher gave me a nod and a thumbs up. It was time.

I looked straight ahead of me, right to the back of the hall, took a deep breath and loud and clear I said (or shouted as my sister Emma told me I was doing so during every rehearsal at home) "THIS IS ST. BARTHOLOMEW'S FAIR" and so began the story of Dick Whittington ... and my love of acting.

My big moment may have passed by in seconds on the makeshift stage at primary school with my one and only line but the nerves and excitement and enjoyment from acting stayed with me. I went on to join the local drama school. Two hours every Monday and Wednesday evening were spent at drama with my friend Katie. I don't remember performing in any plays there but we learnt so much about drama and thoroughly enjoyed ourselves.

A short stint at a Saturday drama school and I was back on the same stage at school but this time in a more prominent position. The stepmother in a rendition of Cinderella named 'Welliella'. It wasn't a golden slipper Cinderella had lost this time but a wellington boot. Marie my friend, a.k.a. the strollerthon bandit, had the lead role of 'Welliella'. I remember having to bring in an 'ugly dress' to wear. My mum gave me one of hers. When my teacher saw it she said "Well done, where did you manage to get that ugly dress?" I didn't have the heart to say it was one of my mum's and that my mum still wore it!

At secondary school I chose drama as a G.C.S.E. option. This was now monologue territory and stage formatting knowledge. I'll never forget playing Mrs Johnson from Blood Brothers alongside another good friend of mine, Serena.

Achieving a B at GCSE, I looked forward to starting my Theatre Studies A Level. I was sure the future stage lights awaited me. I chose Media Studies as I also enjoyed this at GCSE and it seemed to go well with the Theatre Studies. I was carefully mapping out my future in the theatrical or media world. Christian Theology was the last choice of mine. I enjoyed the debates in R.E. and I needed to choose one more A level so I thought I would go with what else I enjoyed.

Just before my first lesson in sixth form, I saw the head of drama across the playground and told him I was looking forward to the course starting. Something he said about there being a great deal of written work made me think he thought I wasn't up to it. So I never turned up to my lessons. I just didn't go. No-one chased me, no-one cared and it was an A level down the drain before it even began. Instead, I just did the other two A Levels I had chosen. Media Studies and Christian Theology. That was the end of my acting career.

I often say now that I did make it as an actress. I act every day of my life as a teacher. As teachers we perform over and over again, changing our style for our audience. In fact, only last week I actually acted for real in class during a game of charades. A student asked me to do 'Afterlife' the television programme by Ricky Gervais. We were only doing charades related to R.E. topics I must point out and afterlife is 100% an R.E. topic. I died dramatically onto the floor before getting up in the afterlife. I'm afraid some students memory of five years of R.E. will probably be this moment only! There were cheers and whoops of 'encore'. Well not exactly encore but they did beg me to replay it the following lesson. Which I of course declined.

I reflect on all of this as another sight beholds me in the queue. Rising out of the concrete bankside of pubs is a white globe. Shakespeare's Globe. Perhaps had my life taken a different turn, or if I hadn't over thought the comment by the drama teacher, I would be performing there.

It looks like a medieval theatre with a thatched roof although it's a relatively new build. It reminds me of Queen Elizabeth's Hunting Lodge in Chingford. A place I once visited on a school trip where I loved imagining I was royalty going from room to room all dressed up with my friend Katie who joined me at the drama club. Coincidentally Katie has recently been reading Shakespeare at a theatre in Los Angeles just this week.

The Hunting Lodge school trip could only be described as fabulous. From eating lunch under one of the oldest trees in Epping Forest to creating dens in the fields and reenacting medieval life. I was acting. I was in a historical place. Pig in s*** comes to mind.

The Globe before me now as I walk the queue is a replica of the Globe that once stood on the same site. The story starts with an actor named James Burbage who lived in the 16th century. James was a travelling actor in the 1550's. Elizabethans enjoyed entertainment away from the daily toil whether that be bear rings or taverns or London's great Bartholomew Fair held every August. The fair I introduced all those eager parents to back in the 1980's during our school play. I didn't even realise it was a real part of history until I started researching for this book. Is it ok to also admit that I didn't know there was a real Dick Whittington a.k.a. Richard Whittington who lived between 1354- 1423. Am I the only one?

As a travelling actor, James would perform in animal baiting arenas or on the side of the road. There were no theatres dedicated to the performance of plays. Entertainment was often violent or religious with animal baiting. Religious plays were the most common (until the ban of mystery plays).

Londoners were keen for entertainment and James Burbage decided he would build a playhouse just for performances. The first of its kind. Ending the street acting and giving actors a real home. Before this time, there simply weren't any. Actors were homeless in their trade.

He signed a lease for some land north of the river and set about going into financial partnership. He was his own architect and builder and decided to make his playhouse round. He named it 'The Theatre' from the Greek Word 'a place for viewing'. The first theatre in London, that all others are named after. Any time you visit a theatre you have James Burbage to thank for its name.

The years brought financial woes, the plague and difficult business times but James continued to run his theatre. Another popped up south of the river on bankside and was called 'The Rose'. Competition didn't help matters, until one day a young William Shakespeare arrived. Shakespeare's writings and acting saved the day for 'The Theatre'.

As the lease began to run out on the land, James' sons began looking for a new lease. In 1598, afraid the theatre would be torn down, they decided to move the theatre across the river to Bankside, piece by piece. New partnerships were made for the new theatre on the south side including Shakespeare.

As the new theatre was built from the old, a decision was made to rename it 'The Globe'. It had room for up to 3,000 people and was a roaring success. That is, however, until 1613 when the Globe burnt down. One year later it was rebuilt. Sadly, just three years later Shakespeare died. Did he ever get over seeing his cherished Globe burn?

1648 saw the government ordering all theatres to be demolished as acting was then considered idolatry.

Fast forward to the 20th century and the lack of acknowledgement of the Globe Theatre along Bankside didn't sit well with some Shakespeare enthusiasts/historians. Eventually it was the actor Sam Wannamaker that organised the campaign to rebuild the Globe. Prince Philip joined him in encouraging the rebuild and lay the first stone. The Royal Family have done so much for London, will we ever know all the stories?

The Globe was built using medieval techniques, but some changes were needed due to fire restrictions and the need for public conveniences.

Wannamaker died before it was completed in 1997 but his children have continued to be strong advocates raising awareness and funds. You may have heard of his daughter, the actress, Zoe Wannamaker.

Her Majesty Queen Elizabeth II and Prince Philip were at the opening ceremony of the new Globe now renamed 'Shakespeare's Globe'.

We shuffle past the white globe, almost illuminated by the now dark night sky. It is getting even later. I check my watch and messages and post a few pictures on Facebook. Everyone seems behind me, 'amazing Laura' 'what an experience' etc. I do feel lucky and privileged to be here. No one else I know has queued. I wonder why I just did it. Something just compelled me to, just like those around us. The nieces behind us are queueing as their aunt begged them. They're not too impressed but they are beginning to say it was probably worth it after all. The time is now 10:30pm.. I'm surprised I haven't felt more hungry. The constant walking, talking and people watching makes the time fly. I have no idea why I ever thought I would want to queue with my head down in a book or series. It's much more interesting being in the present moment and just taking it all in.

Talking about taking it all in, having recently completed a chaplaincy post graduate certificate, a key learning point comes alive on this walk. 'Stop doing and start being.' We are always so busy doing things, sometimes we just need to 'be'. I even fill my leisure time with doing. I must read that book, do the puzzle, go for a walk. Sometimes just being in the moment is all we need. And a bench. A bench is all we need whilst on this queue to end all queues. Thankfully they are in abundance around The Globe giving multiple opportunities to rest and 'just be'.

Overall, I do feel as though I am in the moment in this queue, relishing the history and enjoying the company of those around me. My chaplaincy course also taught me about accompanying. Accompanying people on their journey is an aim of chaplaincy. Here I am accompanying Janet and she is accompanying me. Whilst we just 'be'. We are also on a journey. Although 'accompanying' in the sense of chaplaincy relates to the journey of life rather than an actual journey. It makes for a very peaceful mindset. All worries about it being late, dark and the middle of London simply aren't there as thousands of us are just 'being' and 'accompanying'.

The Thames is lit up by boats and the bridges are still busy with people going about their business. It is a Friday night. It does make you think about every other night when you're at home this whole bustle of life is happening.

As we pass The Globe, a row of three houses stand proud. Imagine living there, looking across to St. Paul's Cathedral across the Thames and on a cobbled street next to The Globe. Lovely, although busy. You would want to keep your curtains closed all the time I would think. I remember once hoovering one Saturday morning in my dressing gown and a student of mine walked past and waved at me through the window. No rest for the wicked. I now enjoy working a few miles further from my house and my current house is well set back from the road so I can enjoy some privacy from the relative fame that comes from teaching.

Cardinal's Wharf is written above the tall three storey white house. It has an interesting connection to royalty. I'm beginning to realise the history all around the queue is intrinsically linked to royalty in one way or another.

This tall white house has a small plaque on it claiming to be 'Wren's house', although it is now believed Christopher Wren, master of architecture, maths, physics and astronomy probably never lived there. The house was built in 1710 on the site of an old tavern that used to be a brothel. The taverns cellars are today incorporated into the house. The house passed different hands from ferrymen to film directors and then more recently the Swedish writer Axel Munthe lived there. In the 1980's Axel's grandson was said to be an 'escort' of Princess Margaret. If cellar walls could talk I'm sure there would be many a story to tell here.

Moving on.

I walk past the Tate Modern thinking it looks quite old and not at all modern. The big sign above it reads 'See great art from around the world'. I'm not one for art galleries. I have been to some exhibitions relating to religious art for my degree but it's not something I have grown to love. I am quite sure that I saw the famous painting 'Christ of Saint John of the Cross' by Salvador Dali. Whether it was on loan from its home place in Glasgow to London or whether I saw it during my PGDE year in Glasgow I can't tell you. (I do mean PGDE by the way. Everyone tries to correct me and say PGCE but my course was a Post Graduate Diploma in Education, not Certificate). I remember seeing this huge painting and thinking 'Wow my Dad has a picture of that on our stairs'.

I have also been to the Louvre in Paris and seen the 'Mona Lisa' by Leonardo Da Vinci. I was underwhelmed with the small size of this painting and was about six rows back from the crowds trying to look at it. I was also about six weeks pregnant and eating more cherry drops than I care to remember to keep the sickness at bay. Poor Paul. We went to Paris for one night and I was probably asleep by 9:30pm and walking around the rest of the time feeling rotten. I do remember one amazing thing about that trip. We ice skated on the Eiffel Tower. It was so unexpected to come across an ice skating rink when we exited the lift and even more unexpected to find out that it was completely free!

Back to the Tate Modern. It used to be a power station which explains why it looks a bit like a workhouse from the outside. I dragged my children around a workhouse in Derbyshire, of course with all the usual parent jokes about leaving them there. Amy recently called my spinach, pepper and asparagus risotto workhouse food. If only she knew.

The Tate reminds me of the workhouse, but it has less windows. Lots of glass at the top, maybe that's the modern bit. Completely missing the point that it holds modern art rather than being modern architecture we look ahead. Are we almost there? Only a couple of hours now surely?

Another bridge... who knew there were so many? This time it's 'The Millenium Bridge'. I remember the wobbly bridge stories when it first opened. As it has now stood firm for 21 years since 2002 when repairs were completed, it is probably unfair to call it the wobbly bridge now.

Opened in the year 2000 by Queen Elizabeth II it was to close two days later due to a lack of shock absorbers. Five million pounds and two years later, it was reopened. The rush of people to cross it was slightly less, all a little more wary than the vast numbers keen to tell everyone they had crossed it on the first day of opening.

It was the first bridge to be built across the Thames in over 100 years. Not a millennial idea but one that had been proposed over a century beforehand. The bridge is now a success, popular with commuters linking St. Paul's Cathedral to the Tate Modern.

Just before the bridge, as we shuffle along next to some railings, a familiar sight beholds me. Padlocks. Not just any padlocks but padlocks telling a story from a moment in time. Hundreds of them are locked onto the railings, engraved with loved ones names and dates. I decide not to use my phone light to explore them further as I'm aware I may be being a little unsociable as I soak up all the sights so I turn to Janet and tell her all about my padlock.

Ten years ago, I found myself drawn to the padlocking trend. Whilst on honeymoon in Bakewell in Derbyshire we came across a bridge that was beginning to fill up with padlocks. Wanting to join in and mark our love forever, Paul went to the local shop, bought a padlock and I carefully engraved Laura and Paul with a heart. We padlocked it to the 16th panel, 3rd row down as we got married on the 16th March. It was one of a few on that particular row and panel.

The bridge is now overflowing with thousands of padlocks. Even padlocks padlocked to padlocks. We return to Bakewell often and we never fail to find ours with the 16/3 rule. It is still there. I'm sure Paul will be pleased to know our love will be forever now as there is no chance of removal of the padlock. The key went missing with the war buttons from the trenches when my purse was lost.

Chapter 12

The Queen's Walk

Sweeping round past yet another pub, the Founders Arms, we come to... you guessed it... another bridge. Blackfriars this time. The queue is snaking all underneath the bridge and it looks as though it's a bit of a squeeze head height wise. I feel like we may have to duck our heads to go underneath to make sure we don't hit our heads. As we approach it, of course, it is a little higher than it looks and no bumped heads to note.

Blackfriars Bridge was first opened in 1769. The then Prime Minister 'William Pitt the Elder' had wanted to name the bridge the 'William Pitt Bridge'. I mean who wouldn't want a bridge named after them? I quite fancy seeing the 'Laura O'Boyle Bridge' one day. He was, as I am sure I would be, unsuccessful in his convincing and the name 'Blackfriars' was given, named after a large Dominican monastery called the Blackfriars which had stood on the site near to the north of the bridge. It was at this monastery that the court hearing between Henry VIII and Catherine of Aragon took place. I'm beginning to realise why the Americans love London and the Royal Family so much. Such history at every turn. Henry VIII and Catherine of Aragon's marriage ended in divorce resulting in Henry VIII founding the Protestant Church of England. Catherine gave a most eloquent speech at the court in Blackfriars. Perhaps next time you are travelling over Blackfriars Bridge you can imagine Catherine pleading in front of her husband saying these words:

"Sir, I beseech you for all the loves that hath been between us, and for the love of God, let me have justice and right, take of me some pity and compassion, for I am a poor woman and a stranger born out of your dominion, I have here no assured friend, and much less indifferent counsel: I flee to you as to the head of justice within this realm. Alas! Sir, wherein have I offended you, or what occasion of displeasure have I designed against your will and pleasure? Intending (as I perceive) to put me from you, I take God and all the world to witness, that I have been to you a true and humble wife, ever conformable to your will and pleasure, that never said or did anything to the contrary thereof, being always well pleased and contented with all things wherein ye had any delight or dalliance, whether it were in little or much, I never grudged in word or countenance, or showed a visage or spark of discontentation. I loved all those whom ye loved only for your sake, whether I had cause or no; and whether they were my friends or my enemies. This twenty years I have been your true wife or more, and by me ye have had divers children, although it hath pleased God to call them out of this world, which hath been no default of me.

And when ye had me at the first, I take God to be my judge, I was a true maid without touch of man; and whether it be true or no, I put it to your conscience. If there be any just cause by the law that ye can allege against me, either of dishonesty or any other impediment to banish and put me from you, I am well content to depart, to my great shame and dishonor; and if there be none, then here I most lowly beseech you let me remain in my former estate, and received justice at your princely hand. The king your father was in the time of his reign of such estimation through the world for his excellent wisdom, that he was accounted and called of all men the second Solomon; and my father Ferdinand, King of Spain, who was esteemed to be one of the wittiest princes that reigned in Spain many years before, were both wise and excellent kings in wisdom and princely behavior. It is not therefore to be doubted, but that they were elected and gathered as wise counsellors about them as to their high discretions was thought meet. Also, as me seemeth there was in those days as wise, as well-learned men, and men of good judgement as be present in both realms, who thought then the marriage between you and me good and lawful Therefore is it a wonder tome what new inventions are now invented against me, that never intended but honesty. And cause me to stand to the order and judgment of this new court, wherein ye may do me much wrong, if ye intend any cruelty; for ye may condemn me for lack of sufficient answer, having no indifferent counsel, but such as be assigned me, with whose wisdom and learning I am not acquainted. Ye must consider that they cannot be indifferent counsellors for my part which be your subjects, and taken out of your own council before, wherein they be made privy, and dare not, for your displeasure, disobey your will and intent, being once made privy thereto. Therefore, I most humbly require you, in the way of charity, and for the love of God, who is the just judge, to spare the extremity of this new court, until I may be advertised what way and order my friends in Spain will advise me to take. And if ye will not extend to me so much indifferent favour, your pleasure then be fulfilled, and to God I commit my case!"

I must say that I feel Blackfriars has a lot more history and relevance as a Bridge name than William Pitt the Elder. I am glad he failed in his mission. What next? The Theresa May Bridge? The Boris Johnson Bridge?

I am now beginning to realise that the bridge that I look at now is not the original. The original Blackfriars Bridge opened in 1769. It was demolished in 1863 due to wear and tear. In 1869 Queen Victoria lay the first stone for the new Blackfriars Bridge that we duck our heads under as we walk to see Queen Elizabeth II lying in state.

As we come out the other side there is a wall mural painted of a Thames view. We are in this section for a brief while, a few minutes perhaps. It allows me time to explore the painting. It's amazing how the painter has painted on to the bricks. A name in the bottom right says 'Jimmy C'. Whether Jimmy C painted it or just added his name as graffiti after I don't know, but whoever the painter was they have a real talent.

Another tunnel around the corner. This time filled with images of various bridges. Very apt. At the end of the tunnel there is a small piece of art work. At first glance it looks like bones but on closer inspection I believe it is various clay pipes found from mudlarking. Engraved on it is a person holding what looks like a bindle. I read:

'Kingdoms may come

Kingdoms may go

Whatever the end may be

Old_father_thames

Keeps rolling along

Down to the mighty sea.'

Old Father Thames it seems was a name given to a cartoon drawing of a filthy vagrant living in the Thames during the Great Stink of the 1850's. No such smells around this evening thank goodness. Not in the queue anyway. I cannot speak for the portaloos. They are beginning to be a law unto themselves.

As we come out of the tunnel firmly on the other side of Blackfriars bridge, we pass... you guessed it ... another pub. The Doggetts. Situated on the corner with another nice seating area with a view of the Thames.

I feel I have left the old Bankside with its bear baiting and brothel houses behind and I am now in posher territory. Black lampposts with intricate designs are now lining the walkway. They say E II R and 1973 on them. It was in 1973 that this section of the Thames path was named 'The Queen's Walk'. We are now on the Queen's Walk in the Queen's Queue. We must be getting closer.

Tall buildings made of concrete and glass surround us. It is warm despite the need for coat and hats. No one is shivering. Everyone is comfortable. There are no complaints of wishing for more layers or wearing the wrong shoes. Everyone is happy and privileged to be part of the queue. It is still a pain to leave 'The Queue' to queue for toilets for five minutes. I hear people saying,

"Look at the long toilet queue, I'm going to wait until the next ones". People still see queues as long if more than ten people in it yet 'this' queue with tens of thousands is fine. How does the mind work like this? Motivation perhaps? Destination? Toilet or the Queen lying in state? The prize at the end of the queue keeps us going.

Just then a woman aged around 60 walks past us in the opposite direction. She is all flustered and stressed. She asks where the beginning of the queue is and we reluctantly tell her around eight hours of queuing behind us. She then asks where she can get a wristband. Again we tell her she needs to join the queue in Southwark Park in order to get the wristband. She looks as though she is going to cry but carries on anyway, walking the queue the wrong way to get to the end. I felt like saying just stand with us, but it wouldn't work. It's not fair on everyone else and besides, she needs her wristband. This isn't a time for friendly favours like letting someone with a basket of two items in Tesco in front of your trolley load, this is 'The Great British Queue' and one must queue like the British, from the start, orderly and with patience.

As I look into a building I notice it says 'Sea Containers'. Did you know the company Sea Containers were paid to leave all of their lights on one night due to a Harry Potter scene where they filmed some flying across the Thames? This is one of the facts I learnt from my husband Paul. He is full of facts, most often due to internet procrastinating but this fact was actually a learnt from life fact.

A recent fact he told me was that the sea doesn't move with the high and low tide but it's the earth that moves. The sea stays in the same place. I liked that one.

Paul used to work at Sea Containers, the shipping company, in this very building I am passing. I didn't know him then but he has often spoken about the 'good old days' of working there. It is now a posh hotel and poshly priced accordingly. A 12th floor bar, boutique restaurant and decor to match a ships interior all adding to the ambience. A nice place to stay for an exploration of the Southbank. Apparently the company is somehow now linked to The Orient Express. If only he had stayed with them I might be living the life right now with days out on the Orient Express! He also worked at Burberry's for a while. Again, the perks would have been somewhat ideal. Now he works for Tumble Tots. The odd free children's coordination toy is about it.

A major perk though is he gets all the school holidays off, as do I. I remember the first year. It was awful. I couldn't believe he was around at home for six whole weeks! It took some adjusting. I remember feeling a kinship with a lady I once knew called Rae. When her husband retired, she used to make him a packed lunch and send him off to the summer house in the garden each morning. There he would read the paper, do a crossword, some gardening, read a book, eat his lunch, make tea and return home mid afternoon. I remember feeling something like this was needed during Paul's first summer off. By the second summer though, the perks had kicked in and we all got used to all the extra family time together. Now we wouldn't be without it.

A red telephone box with Sea Containers written on it stands outside the hotel. People begin taking selfies and photos. I forget that there are people in this queue from all over the country and so it is a sightseeing tourist queue for many. Red telephone boxes, black taxis and red London buses are all getting photographed.

Following the black lampposts of the Queen's Walk along the Thames, standing proudly in its own right next to the Sea Containers Hotel, is the famous OXO Tower.

My youngest daughter Emily recently went to a birthday party there for a meal. She was aged eight. I thought what a posh place for a party and how wonderful for her to see the views. It turned out that her friend's dad worked there, hence the party location. I'm still yet to go but again, something for the to do list.

The famous OXO Tower is an interesting one. Advertising on buildings wasn't allowed when it was built. A clever marketing strategy involved sticking to the law and placing no advertising boards on the outside of the building. Instead, some strategically designed windows that spelt out OXO were installed and remain to this day.

The OXO Tower was originally a power station supplying electricity to the Royal Mail post office, built in the 19th century. The Liebig Extract of Meat Company took over in the 1920's. The tower itself isn't accessible to the public but the rest of the building now houses flats, shops and the restaurant mentioned above.

I see the OXO Tower as somewhat of a landmark along the London skyline, yet it isn't listed. You would assume it was but no. Maybe not historical enough being relatively new at only a couple of hundred years old.

We meander on. The path is getting wider, more tree lined and is looking like the London Southbank that I know. Benches aplenty and more portaloos. I'm beginning to think this book should be called 'Bridges, Benches, Pubs and Toilets'.

The Queen's Walk signs add to the royal feel. Tourist information is in abundance and I notice a useful guide board pointing out how long it is from here to walk to various sights. Apparently 15 minutes to Westminster. Turns out that 15 minutes is about four and a half hours this evening. It's now half past ten. I'm beginning to predict we will be there by 1am. I was wrong.

Amongst the black Queen's Walk lampposts that remind me of something out of Mary Poppins, there are further things to read and see. A tribute to the BT Tower and telecommunications as a whole. I probably haven't thought about this for 35 years since I went, but I now remember a school trip to the BT Tower. Lots of buttons to press and walkie talkie style communications.

Talking of walkie talkies, it's been great to see them in the recent phenomena that is 'Stranger Things' which is based in the 80's. I once had a set that was probably one of my favourite ever childhood toys. When we used to drive all the way to Spain, (Six of us in a Maestro or Space Cruiser with no air conditioning) my Dad used to flash his hazards and my Uncle Dennis behind would get as close as he safely could to our car whilst driving on the autoroute of France and they would communicate with each other through the walkie talkies. "Ready for a stop yet Perce? I've got two here needing the toilet. Over."

"I think we can push on to the next aire. Over." No need for mobile phones. Good old fashioned fun. When we did make it to the aire, we used to get out of our hot car with relief. My cousins used to get out of their air conditioned car and jump straight back in. Back when life was simple.

So, shuffling along, we pass the National Theatre. I'm not an expert on the Southbank. There are big red banners telling me that this is what we are passing. I look around to locate it and realise that it is the concrete building next to us that I thought was a multi storey car park.

The foundation stone was laid by the Queen Mother in 1951, the then Queen Elizabeth. It was to be another 25 years before the theatre was finally finished and open to the public.

Meanwhile the National Theatre as a company had grown to a reputable reputation, using a theatre next to Waterloo Station whilst it awaited its own premises. The growth of the company is due to the Director of the National Theatre, Laurence Olivier. It is his statue I see before me standing proudly outside the theatre as we walk past.

Today there are three theatres which hold various opportunities for productions, as well as opportunities for children, the youth and local community organisations.

The clientele of people we pass is changing. The office drinkers along the Shad Thames has now turned into a younger, more hip and trendy mix. Baggy trousers, dungarees, tattoo's, interesting hairstyles and skateboards under arms or under feet go past.

We pass Waterloo Bridge. The second one. The first was built in 1817 and demolished in the 1930's with the current Waterloo Bridge finally being completed in 1945.

We soon come across plenty of skateboarders as we the queuers look on and take it all in. The undercroft of the Southbank Centre is full of cool looking trendy youngsters skateboarding their Friday night away. Not only is it the hangout for hip skateboarders but it's obviously a place for budding graffiti artists to leave their mark. The walls, pillars and ceiling are covered in street graffiti. I can't make out what any of it says but it certainly looks like a place that is far too cool for the likes of me. Southbank Skatepark at 11pm on a Friday night. Get me.

I think about edging in and taking a selfie for my kids but I'm getting tired now and can't be bothered to do anything extra other than put one small step in front of the other.

Just beyond the skateboarding we pass The Royal Festival Hall. It is a key moment in the queue. This is where I see Westminster for the first time.

"Look it's just over there! We've made it!" I hear myself saying. "It wont be long now, maybe two hours?" What I didn't know then was that the queue went beyond Westminster then back on itself and the final surprise of all, The Westminster Snake for a final two hours of queueing in the gardens of Westminster Hall.

Not knowing timings and queue snakes ahead, I feel upbeat and motivated. It's now almost 11pm. I've been queuing for eight hours or like I have called it many times 'very slow walking'. I check my texts. Mum checking I'm ok and she's going to bed now but to ring if I need anything. She's transferred the money for my cab home. My cousins Martine and Felicity on our cousin chat have a plethora of messages that I don't have the battery to go through now but I will catch up on tomorrow. Amy and Emily have sent texts,

"Where are you now?"

"What time will you be home?"

I text a quick message.

"Can see Westminster. Not long to go now hopefully!" and turn my phone off again ready for the next leg of my journey.

Chapter 13
Bag Drop

The Queen's Walk is probably the busiest part of the walk. It is busy enough for the queue to be held back by stewards. After all the slow shuffling of feet we are at a standstill for a good 10-15 minutes. Sods law there are no benches next to us for this prolonged stoppage. This feels more like a queue I am used to. People begin looking left and right over the heads in front of them to see what the hold up is. I ask the nearest steward. It is simply numbers and crowds.

Revellers swarm the area and in order to let them move between street food stalls and bars and skateboards, the queue is held until there is sufficient space in front to move and still leave a gap for sales. The food stall vendors must be making a good amount with the thousands of queuers these past few days. Some people look like they are trying to cash in on the queue. Posters and postcards of the Queen are set up along benches "£5 for 5 postcards!" I wonder where they managed to get their stock from so as to benefit from the queue. It's amazing how opportunities arise and people look to money making schemes.

However, they don't look like they are selling many. Not from our section of the queue anyway. Maybe they did a better trade earlier in the day.

As expected no one is bored. There is plenty of people watching going on and sights to behold.

A railway bridge is busy taking trains over the Thames. I wonder if Carole has ever worked on railway bridges. Carole is my eldest daughter's sister and my stepdaughter once upon a time although I didn't quite marry her Dad. She is an engineer on the railways so it's probably quite likely that she has worked on the bridges. I'll have to bore her with all I've learnt about the London Bridges some time in the future.

Standing tall in front of us is the Millenium Wheel. I've never quite understood the engineering of how the pods are attached on one side and then on the other as it makes its way back down. A question Carole might be able to answer given her background.

I have never been on the Millenium Wheel. Over thinking leads to a bit of panic and worry. There is a smaller version in Great Yarmouth which I also refused to go on. One day perhaps although I do like my feet on solid ground. As they are now. Aching and a bit heavy. I think again as to how nice this queue would be if there was something like a land train that took us from Southwark Park along the Thames to Westminster Hall. Perhaps a guide telling us the sights as we pass. Maybe it's time to bring back the ferrymen and they could have ferried us up and down the Thames. Of course, there are ferrymen today. They are called the Thames Clippers, but they are not for us queuers. We must queue the old-fashioned way.

I wonder if there is any corruption in the queue. Wristbands sold or backhanders to stewards to move up the queue. I doubt it. It doesn't look like anyone here would want to do the wrong thing but you just never know.

I remember a story Paul once told me. I think it's real although I don't know his source. I never know his source. I just choose to believe some of what he says and sometimes none of what he says. So the story that comes to mind as I contemplate corruption and cheats was that there was a car park somewhere in the UK by a historical site. Every day a man turned up and took the cash payment from those using the car park. He did so for 25 years, then retired and left. It turned out the car park was nothing to do with him. He just took the money.

I think good on him! He worked every day, no one could say he was a shirker. Yet he was taking money that was otherwise a free car park. If it was me I would surely get caught the first day but what an eye for an opportunity! He was similar to the ferrymen trying to charge people to cross the ice. It wasn't their ice to do so. I guess where there's a will there's a way.

I begin to think about the money makers en route. I really should have bought some postcards and definitely the cake from the younger children earlier on. Enterprise should be rewarded.

The steward moves aside and we are once more on our way. Onwards we move through the food stalls as we bend down towards the left, away from the Millenium Wheel and away from the liquid history of the Thames. Through a small park with walls in abundance for sitting on. It's funny how I now know the Southbank in terms of its benches and walls.

We come out onto a posh road with tall office buildings and hotels. Belvedere Road. The road is closed to traffic but we all stick to the pavement, hugging the buildings as we walk. It is eerily quiet compared to the Thames waterfront we have just left behind.

Various groups of media are set up and interview the queue at different moments for their various live segments. I'm not approached to talk but I enjoy listening to others. They still sound so enthusiastic and cheerful despite the long hours and tiredness.

As we approach the end of Belvedere Road the queue heads to the right. The beginning of Westminster Bridge. At last we seem to be crossing the river. A sign pointing in the opposite direction to the queue says, 'bag drop'.

My bag is small enough to be allowed into Westminster Hall but Janet's isn't. Nor is the bag of the aunt walking along with us. They decide to head off and follow the signs for the bag drop with one of the nieces whilst me and the other niece wait on the corner. And wait we did. I'm not exaggerating when I say thousands of queuers went ahead of us, along with David Q and his daughter and the louder bunch behind us. W e waited and waited and waited.

We ended up asking a steward where the bag drop was. He told us it was about a ten minute walk away from the queue. So that meant ten minutes there, ten minutes back let alone the time it took to queue to drop the bag off. I'll never understand why it was such a detour from the queue. The roads were now shut so a makeshift marquee bag drop a bit closer would have made more sense. Then again, security. Everything is carefully planned.

The bag drop was by St. Thomas' Hospital. An iconic hospital that was first founded in the 1100's and named after St. Thomas Becket. Originally a safe haven for the poor, sick and homeless.

As with many London landmarks, the hospital was renamed after Thomas the Apostle and the original building and site changed over the years. There is, in true London style, some historical aspects still to see and you can visit the old original operating theatre, known to be the oldest in Europe. You can find it between Tower and London Bridges.

Today's building and site was opened in 1871 by Queen Victoria who also laid the first foundation stone in 1868. Various enhancements and rebuildings have taken place. In 1967 Queen Elizabeth II opened a new 13 storey wing and 5 storey outpatient block.

Linking to Queen Victoria and Queen Elizabeth II, I feel I should mention two other significant women associated with St. Thomas' Hospital. It was at this hospital that Florence Nightingale opened the world's first nursing school and became known for wandering the wards at night with a lamp to keep the patient's company. Florence was forward thinking in terms of disease and infection and realised that patients were not dying from what they entered hospital with, but from the infection within the hospital itself. She became an advocate for washing hands and cleanliness which became key to improving standards.

Sometimes in the past I have felt like Florence Nightingale. Not because I am a nurse. But because I have crept around in the dark in a long white nightie. Only not holding a candle but a torch.

I remember being on holiday in Yorkshire and creeping outside in my Past Times ensemble with a torch in order to have a cigarette. If anyone saw me from another cottage window they would have definitely have thought they were seeing a ghost from 100 years ago.

Talking of Yorkshire, as well as our lovely family holidays in Spain, we always had a week in Yorkshire too. My friend Katie's family were good friends with my family so we always went together and sometimes with my cousin Felicity's family too. Long muddy walks, pub lunches, evenings around the open fire making towers out of playing cards. Not everyone's cup of tea but to me... bliss.

Back to St. Thomas' and the other significant woman associated with the hospital is Mary Seacole. In the gardens of the hospital there stands a statue of Mary in remembrance.

Mary is known for being the Jamaican nurse who helped soldiers regardless of side during the Crimean War. Despite Mary's vast nursing experience, she was refused entry as an army nurse. She believed this was due to racial prejudice. She went ahead to help the war effort anyway (good for her) and is fondly remembered for her nursing care.

As I write this the NHS is celebrating 75 years. Who knows what the future holds for our National Health Service. I think back to the statues outside the Angel pub. Dr Salter was probably one of the first to provide an NHS, helping poor patients free of charge.

Equal service for all regardless of wealth and poverty is at the heart of the NHS. Some people love it, most people want it improved, some people want to make big changes. Regardless, everyone has a personal story to tell, some positive, some not so.

For me, the NHS has saved my life twice in an emergency. Once when I presented at A & E in excruciating pain in 2009. I had pancreatitis. A week's stay in hospital, followed by a scheduled operation and I was as right as rain.

Another time was in 2012 when they predicted I would have pre-eclampsia and admitted me as soon as I showed signs. 15 days later on the maximum dose of blood pressure medicine they could give me they awaited for my blood pressure to drop below 250/150 in order to carry out an emergency C section, saving both mine and Emily's life. The monitoring of my blood pressure with 24/7 1:1 care I will forever be grateful for.

The every 2 minute monitoring went to every 15 minute monitoring for the first 24 hours after giving birth as they adjusted my medicines. You honestly couldn't pay for better care. I hope and pray that the NHS continues for the next 75 years and receives funding to do so. Paul tells me the NHS is the biggest employer in Britain with over two million employees. I think he's right with this fact.

Back to the corner of Belvedere Road and as we wait and wait and wait, watching thousands go ahead of us we feel a little disheartened. We felt we were there and now we wonder will they ever return from the bag drop?

I try to rationalise with myself that they will indeed return and we will continue on our way. My friend Marie's dad Bern once told her a story to help her patience in traffic jams. He said to look around at all the skeletons in cars around you. As you will see there are none. So don't worry, you will not be here forever. I often think of this when I find myself getting impatient.

I look ahead to the other side of the bridge. Standing tall and proud and as though it has always been there is Big Ben. Another iconic London landmark. An apt time to report on the time. The clock reads 11.45pm. Nearly midnight.

As I look across the bridge to Big Ben I try to spot the tilt. I can't see it. The experts say that the naked eye can't see it, yet it is there. In 10,000 years time it will be like the leaning Tower of Pisa. I wonder who will be here looking at it then. Will it even still be standing or long since demolished with the second, third and fourth replacement just like some of the other London Bridges?

The current Big Ben has stood proud for over 160 years. The bell itself is called Big Ben. Named after Benjamin Hall who oversaw the installation of the bell in his position as the 'First Commissioner of Works'. It is 13.5 tons and 2.2 metres high.

The tall tower that houses the bell is called the Elizabeth Tower, named after... you guessed it 'Queen Elizabeth II', renamed to celebrate the Diamond Jubilee.

The tower has 334 steps leading up to the main bell, Big Ben and four other bells known as the quarter bells. The main bell is of course the second one having replaced the first. The first bell got a large crack in it after ten months of testing and was broken up to be recycled.

The second bell began chiming in July 1859, only to cease service just a few months later in October 1859 when once more a large crack was found. The largest of the quarter bells took on the duty of chiming instead of Big Ben until 1863 when it was decided to turn Big Ben slightly and start hammering on a non cracked part of the bell. This worked and the second Big Ben has been in service ever since. So, the great bell at the top of the Elizabeth Tower is cracked and turned out of position. Who knew?

The clock itself was made by Frederick Dent in 1854. Clockmakers today maintain the clock as well as all the clocks in Westminster. Back in 1854, the clock used to be wound by hand and so two men were employed five hours a day, three days a week to do the winding. This happened for 50 years. Not a bad job.

Today the clock is kept clean by abseilers. This fact reminds me of the scene in the recent Mary Poppins Returns film where Mary Poppins saves the day by floating past Big Ben with her umbrella and changing the time so as to save the Banks family from certain bankruptcy. As far as sequels go this is brilliant. I might even go as far to say better than the first.

Brought back into the moment I see Janet coming around the corner. They walk towards us, bagless and still chatting away. As we join the queue again the nieces decide it isn't fair that we have lost our place and start to walk 'past the queuers' in a quick march to try and find our original space. Well. I joined in. What choice did I have? But I definitely felt like a queue jumper at this stage. Walking past thousands of queuers all eyeing us with suspicion. Were we allowed to rejoin where we had stepped out? At all other times in the queue we were allowed to do so. Everyone did so. For toilet breaks, coffee breaks etc. Surely we could do the same with the bag drop? Yet the amount of queuers that had passed us made me feel a little uneasy.

As we frogmarched past, I realised that the queue didn't go over Westminster Bridge as I thought (and hoped) it would. I honestly thought that was it. We were almost there at Westminster Hall. The bag drop only adding to my belief we were at the end.

However, as we began our walk over the bridge we never quite made it to the river. Before we got to the river the queue veered left down some steps and along the river looking over to Westminster Hall on the other side.

A steward tried to stop us at one point and I said,

"We took half an hour at the bag drop so we are trying to find our place in the queue". He let us through. That eased my conscience. We weren't pushing in. We were just finding our place again after the detour. As we found 'our people' a cheer broke out and we were welcomed back into our rightful place to continue queuing.

Chapter 14

Hearts for Covid

Now established back in our original place in the queue, I take the opportunity to turn my phone on and take a selfie with Westminster in the background. It is darker along this path than the previous sections. There are no bars, pubs or skateboarders. Just us queuers and the Thames. There is a chill in the air but I have red warm cheeks. I think the tiredness is keeping me warm.

I worry momentarily that the cold fresh night air might trigger my asthma and pull up a scarf over my mouth. I think if there was a mattress on the floor I would probably be asleep in minutes at this stage. I've always been an early bird needing lots of sleep. The adventure of the queue is exhilarating but also tiring.

We head towards Lambeth Bridge where stewards are once again checking wrist bands. They are as jovial and upbeat as the stewards in Southwark Park.

"Nearly there now!"

"Well done." A few words of encouragement are enough to make us smile and continue on our way.

There is an element of guilt of course. What about those that run marathons for charity? Those that queue for hours for basic life essentials? We aren't worthy of applause. We have chosen to do this. Yet the feeling that each one of us represents thousands before us stays with me. We are doing this on behalf of so many past and present. I almost expect these lively motivators to give us all a medal. They are doing an excellent job. Where they get their energy from I don't know.

Just before we get to the end of the riverside path between Westminster Bridge and Lambeth Bridge, we pass a wall. This isn't just any wall. It isn't a wall for us to rest our feet like so many we have passed and utilised.

It is a wall covered in thousands of red hearts.

I hold my breath and feel a shiver. This is the Covid Memorial Wall. I'd read about this and seen it on the news, not knowing exactly where it was or that we would be passing it after quite an emotional ten hour walk.

It is the quietest stretch of path we have walked on. No revellers and just the midnight shimmering of the Thames with Big Ben and Westminster in the background.

Each heart shines in front of us representing a life lost during the Covid 19 Pandemic. It represents a time of fear, uncertainty and suspicion. Wiping our shopping, wearing masks, staying home, watching daily news updates with disbelief that this was happening in the modern world.

Schools closed, work from home, cars idle on driveways with nowhere to go. People singing from their balconies in Italy, clapping on their doorsteps in the UK for the NHS and wildlife resurfacing and healing where humans no longer walked.

A respiratory illness spreading through the world like wildfire. The government paying everyone's wages to stay at home. The year was 2020.

I felt as though I was living through a modern day plague. It was hard to comprehend and make sense of it all. There was a mixture of modern medicine with old fashioned sacrifices. Old wives tales spread online. Leave onions outside the door of those with Covid to catch the germs, put onions in your socks, leave your hair wet, eat chicken soup.

People crossed the road if they saw you coming. I remember walking in the forest behind my house and saying to Paul,

"I don't think we catch this from close contact, I think it's in the air". It is hard to comprehend now that we have lived through it but at the time it was the strangest thing.

Yet this wasn't the first time people had stayed home to save lives. There was an eerie feel that history was repeating itself.

Covid 19 along with all its lockdowns, deaths and sacrifices reminded me of a historical plague village in Derbyshire that has held my attention since I first visited in 1994 aged 15 with Katie and her family. Since then I have revisited numerous times, even insisting on having my honeymoon in Derbyshire and spending the day at the plague village. My children have been dragged around there now year upon year since 2013. The village is called Eyam and this is it's story.

The year is 1665. Plague is wreaking havoc in London. Deaths, disease and despair are part of daily life. We now know that those that lived on London Bridge were mostly spared likely due to the ventilation on the bridge. However, for one small village in Derbyshire it is about to unleash itself with dire consequences.

A young tailors assistant, George Viccars, has just received a cloth delivery from London. It is damp and so he hangs it out to dry. Within the next month, three of the household where he lived and worked have died from the plague. Throughout the next 18 months the plague spread rapidly throughout the village with whole households wiped out.

The then vicar, William Mompesson, took a leading position to contain the plague. Church services were held outdoors to protect the vulnerable. No one knew quite how the plague was spreading although there was talk of plague seeds being passed from one person to the next. Mompesson suggested that all of the village 'lock down'. He suggested they do not go anywhere in order to save the souls of the nearby villages and the rest of the midlands.

Eyam residents did as they were told led by the Reverend and his wife Catherine Mompesson. Knowing they were sentencing many to a certain death, they chose to sacrifice themselves in order to stop the plague from spreading.

Leaving money in holes in vinegar at the boundary stone, they awaited provision supplies from the nearby village of Stoney Middleton. Vinegar was used as a disinfectant for the coins. No one ventured in to Eyam and no one ventured out. Overall, 260 out of the population of 800 perished.

Makeshift graves were dug in gardens to avoid the spread. Walking around Eyam today, you will find plaques, graves and a museum dedicated to all those that lost their lives.

Some of those that survived still have blood relatives living in the village today. Catherine Mompesson's grave can be seen in grounds of St. Lawrence's Church, Eyam. Nearby to it stands the old Saxon Cross. The cross dates back to the early ninth century. It is sure to have been the sight of many plague victims and prayers of desperate family victims.

Two stories from the village always hold my attention. Firstly, that of Elizabeth Hancock. Living with her husband and six children just on the edge of Eyam in Riley, Elizabeth's family managed to avoid the plague until August 1666. Alas, within the space of eight days, all of her six children and her husband died.

Elizabeth herself carried the bodies and dug the graves, each time returning to find another one knocking on death's door. These graves are known as 'The Riley Graves' and are situated in a field on the edge of Eyam today. They are protected by the National Trust. The heartache and devastation of Elizabeth is too much to bear. This was just one story.

The other story that captures my attention on each visit to Eyam is that of Emmott Sydall. Aged just 22 when the plague broke out in the village, she sacrificed meeting up with her fiancé Rowland Torre from nearby Stoney Middleton. They would meet at a distance and shout across to each other instead in order to protect their families and villages.

Emmott watched on as five of her siblings and her father died. She had seemed to be immune when the plague finally struck her in April 1666. Rowland continued to go to their meeting place in the hope she would return. The day the village opened Rowland was the first one in looking for Emmott, only to find that she had died some months earlier.

A plaque is all that is left of the Sydall family today and can be found in the village of Eyam commemorating the family that lost their lives. George Viccar's house opposite the Sydall family home also still stands. Elizabeth Hancock's farmhouse is no longer there but her family graves are.

Some years ago Emmott Sydall's family home was for sale. I must admit to being tempted to move to Eyam and live there. With my Past Times nightie I think I would have fitted in to the history of the house pretty well.

Under the Reverend Mompesson's guidance, containing the plague in Eyam worked and the spread came to an end in the Midlands.

In today's global society, it is much harder to contain infectious diseases. Over 227,000 thousand people in the U.K. have Covid 19 recorded on their death certificate. Some died *with* Covid and some died *of* Covid.

The sheer numbers are shocking to see as a visual. There are over 220,000 red hearts on the wall as we pass. The heart wall stretches for 500 metres, heart after heart after heart. We are all silent as we walk past looking and reading names and messages. We begin to share our own stories of loved ones that suffered and died during the pandemic.

I begin to speak of Debbie. My aunt. My uncle's wife. My cousin's mum. My mum's sister-in-law. Debbie was always my pretty, fashionable, trendy aunt. At least to me. She always looked well with her hair styled and make up on. I didn't see her regularly but she was one of our family. A loved and cherished member of our family who had been there since my childhood. Facebook kept us in touch as is often the way with larger families these days. She was always there. Her presence at the family gatherings when I was a child became her presence on my Facebook posts. She commented on everything and liked all my happy news. We were not only aunt and niece but firm Facebook friends.

Debbie began to have some health problems a few weeks before contracting Covid. Sadly, her Covid story mirrored many that we saw on the news. Hospital admittance, oxygen and then ventilation. We all prayed for her.

I had joined an online rosary group during the pandemic and we prayed for Debbie night after night. There were moments of hope and moments of despair. We prayed for my Uncle Danny and my cousins Billy, Sophie and Emma. The stories we had seen on the news were no longer news stories. It was happening within our family.

Sadly, our prayers weren't answered in the way we had hoped. Debbie was just 55 years old when she died in hospital with Covid. She left behind my Uncle Danny, her son Billy aged 25, her daughter Sophie aged 15 and her looked after daughter Emma aged 12.

My Uncle Danny began to write poems to remember the love of his life and put into words his feelings of grief. He has kindly allowed me to share one below.

"Debbie Mottram knocked on the pearly gates

And Peter came to say

What a beautiful angel you are

You're welcome here today.

He took her gently by the hand

And led her nervously inside

A bright light shone in the big blue sky

And her smile became so wide.

Two figures walked into her path

It was her beloved mum and dad

They cuddled and cried for a long long time

Tears of joy and of sad.

I have left my beautiful family behind she said

They miss me all so much

Is it possible to reach out one more time

And let them feel my touch.

Unfortunately not said mum and dad

But you really should not be sad

They all love each other so so much

And for that we must be glad.

We are in a special place right now

And we will watch over them from above

We cannot reach out for that longed for touch

But they will always feel our love.

You have had a perilous journey here

Let me show you to your bed

Close your eyes and rest said Alice and Ron

And lay down your sleeping head.

Tomorrow is another day

For them and us and you

We will all love and comfort each other

In everything we do.

They will always have you in their hearts

And they will be in yours too

That beautiful family you left behind

Will never stop loving you."

The loss of Debbie is profound. Lifechanging for my uncle and cousins who miss her presence daily. Debbie is just one of those hearts on the Covid memorial wall. Another 220,000 husbands, wives, partners and children are left behind grieving with my Uncle Danny. Each one of these thousands of hearts have a family and a story behind them.

We will always remember Debbie. We will always mourn her loss. We will always be thankful for her life and love. Rest in peace Debbie. We will meet again.

Ending with the covid hearts is poignant, moving and emotional. As the queue moves on past the covid hearts and up the steps onto Lambeth Bridge I feel that we have ended our journey in many ways, despite needing to still cross over the bridge

We are now finally walking across the Thames. I can't count how many bridges we have walked past. To walk over one feels like victory. This one is the second Lambeth Bridge. Of course it is the second one, the first bridges are all long gone now.

The first was built in 1860 and was closed to vehicles in 1910. In 1932 the bridge we walk across now was built. It was of course opened by royalty. This time King George V did the honours. Queen Elizabeth II's grandfather. Unlike the OXO Tower (I can't get over that one) it is a listed building. So, just across this final listed building bridge and we are there, at Westminster. It is now ten to one in the early morning. My cheeks are still unusually red from the tiredness and cold yet they feel warm. I take out my phone and record a little video to send to my girls.

"Hi girls! We've just crossed over the last bridge and I've been going ten hours. I think it's just one to two hours to go. It's the last bit of queue now. Bye!"

Climbing down the steps on the other side of Lambeth Bridge into Westminster Gardens, I thought we would be met by security in the gardens of Westminster, but no, that is still two hours away. Instead, the final hurdle is in sight. Rows upon rows of queueing just like in Southwark Park. So near and yet so far. Hello Westminster Snake.

Chapter 15
The Westminster Snake

We are met by rows upon rows of people snaking up and down in Victoria Tower Gardens. A royal park leading up to the buildings of Westminster. The final hurdle.

The hardest part of the Southwark Snake was the viewpoint not changing for two hours. I am hopeful, but wrong, that this snake will be quicker.

As we are about to embark upon the snake we are offered blankets. Brand new blankets are being taking out of their wrapping as they are handed out to queuers. I politely decline. Once again I feel unworthy. Can I manage a few hours in the cold night air? The answer is yes. I expected this and I have my jumper and coat and hat. Fair enough, some people just joining the queue as nighttime falls will be in the cold all night long for 12 hours. The blankets will be more than just a little extra warmth to them. Some of those around us take the blankets and some do not.

Bottles of water are also being handed out. I know some complained at this provision due to the many homeless needing warmth and shelter in London. I can only assume it is part of the event planning risk assessment. Thousands of queuers are being cared for so as to avoid first aid treatment. Preventative rather than reactive. Of course, there are also first aid stations. The death of a monarch requires precise planning and a multi agency approach. Just thinking back to the isolated bag that we found. It was reported and within only a minute or two police were there. It wasn't a coincidence that they were so close. It was all part of the planning.

We walk past a children's playground and find ourselves once more on the familiar rubber mats that we encountered in Southwark Park. Somehow we have become slightly separated from some of our group so instead of queuing with them, we wave to them as we snake up and down past each other. Well to start with we do, then it becomes a nod and then a smile. Enthusiasm drops a little with the mundaneness of the snake. After around 30 minutes of pretty boring slow snake walking, I look at a monument we have passed and it feels as though we have made no progress at all. It really is the most disheartening part of the queue. You keep moving, yet the scenery remains the same and you seem to get nowhere. Once again it gives ample opportunity to focus in on what there is to look at.

The monument that I feel I am not getting any further away from looks like a mini stone cathedral. I know a little about architecture and artwork thanks to my study of the Romanesque period for my degree. This building, however, is carved intricately in gothic style.

It is the Buxton Memorial Fountain.

A drinking fountain designed to honour the abolition of slavery and to commemorate the MP Thomas Powell Buxton's role in this. Designed by Buxton's son it was created in 1865 and was moved to its current position in 1957. It does remind me of my Church aesthetics 10,000 word dissertation I wrote back in 2001. I still love visiting architectural wow factor places of worship now. I just never seem to find or indeed make the time.

The Westminster snake differs from the Southwark snake. As we approach an hour of snaking up and down we come across portaloos in the snake. You don't need to step outside of the queue for these ones, you can just go as you queue whilst staying in the snake. Very handy. Although once I'm in I realise that it feels a bit risky with hundreds of queuers a stones throw from the door. Again it is very dark inside. I wonder why they aren't made with lights. You can't see a thing. I guess that might not be a bad thing after days of queuers using them.

One of the most difficult things about a snake queue is that there are no benches to sit down for a rest so it is just slow walking up and down and up and down and up and down.

After about an hour I realise we are about halfway through the snake. I take my woolly hat off to feel the fresh air as I'm still warm with the tiredness. We continue chatting as we have done throughout, grateful to be in the last section.

I begin to wonder what it will be like seeing the Queen lying in state. I imagine it will be a quick walking past and we are out. I decide that I will stop and make the sign of the cross and bow my head out of respect. I hope that I take in every moment so that I can remember it and share with my family.

I begin to make predicted times to Paul so he can watch on the TV at home. I may not have mentioned but there is a live stream of the lying in state. I am going to be on the TV.

Suddenly there is progress. I can see a few snake lines ahead. There seems to be rows upon rows behind us and only around six rows in front of us and then no more snaking up and down. Instead, the queue snakes around a green and the edge of Westminster. We are nearly there.

I also notice people 'rejoining' the queue.

"Where have they been?" I wonder to myself. Then I point out to Janet.

"Look, there's benches all along the river. We could have taken turns during the snake to rest our feet!" What a shame we hadn't noticed before. Two hours of queuing could have been at least an hour of sitting. Never mind.

Blankets are being collected back in. I notice some holding on to them and squeezing them into their small bags. Everyone loves a freebie. My forte is the hot chocolate sachets from hotels.

We are told to discard any food and drinks into large waste bags held open for us.

I panic.

I haven't yet eaten my Red Hot Monster Munch. It's 1.15am and probably the last thing I feel like eating but I will not let them go to waste. I open them and eat every one. They can have my crisp packet but not my crisps. I momentarily think back to my Grandma and the night that she died. I feel her presence with me. How I would love to visit her and tell her all about visiting the Queen lying in state and the story of the queue. Somehow I know I don't need to tell her all about it. She knows.

Further items need sacrificing. Janet has a hand cream that must go, others have lip balms or mascara. All cannot be taken through to Westminster Hall. A wall becomes covered in all sorts of make up, toiletries and perfumes as queuers empty their bags. I wonder how many people read the restricted items list. I did but then I think I'm a bit of an over planner wanting to get things right.

As queuers are emptying their bags of what they deemed as queueing necessities, there are six men watching us. Not any old six men but these are 'The Burghers of Calais'.

The Burghers of Calais are sculptures of six men from Calais who sacrificed themselves during the 100 year war back in the 14th century.

They offered to give themselves up for death if the rest of the town could be spared. Thanks to King Edward III's wife, Queen Philippa, the Burghers were also spared their lives. To commemorate them, sculptures were commissioned.

Auguste Rodin was the sculptor. He completed them in 1889 and they stood outside Calais Town Hall. Rodin made casts of the sculptures and it is one of these casts that we walk past at the end of the queue. Placed in Victoria Tower Gardens in 1914, the Burghers have now been part of the tourist trail for over 100 years. It seems apt that we see these figures of sacrifice before visiting our Queen lying in state in order to pay respect and thanks for her sacrifice.

As food and supplies are discarded, we round the final bend. Dazzling bright white lights blind me for a moment as I take in the scene in front of me. From the dark shuffling queue we are now in very different territory. It reminds me of queuing for Santa Claus. Suddenly you round a bend and find yourselves in the North Pole with elves hard at work. It always invokes a gasp of surprise even though it is what you are there to see.

Instead of elves hard at work, in this case it is police officers. The sight in front of me is of huge lights shining down onto the scene below. You would never know it was night time. There are literally hundreds upon hundreds of police officers. The security is like that at an airport. Walk through sensors, bag checks and body searches. Only it isn't a load of security workers at their job as you get at an airport. The whole security operation is police. I have never seen anything like it.

I walk through the first sensor arch before emptying my bag into a tray. A police officer picks up my blue asthma pump and takes it out of its box and opens it. He lifts the spray can out then pieces it back together. I have never been under so much scrutiny.

I decide to make small talk. I ask him

"So, I hear David Beckham was here earlier. Did you see him?"

"No I didn't" came the reply.

"Oh that's a shame" I responded and moved on to collect my bag.

I'm sure he had heard a similar question many times. It's almost like a cab journey. You can't help but ask if they are busy. It must be draining to hear the same thing over and over.

He was part of the Metropolitan Police 'Operation London Bridge'. The Queen's death was the biggest policing operation ever delivered with police from all over the UK supporting the operation. From convoy protection from Scotland to England to crowd control to diplomatic protection to queue safety to lying in state security, Operation London Bridge has been worked on for many years.

The Gold Commander, Deputy Assistant Commissioner Jane Connors, had full responsibility for everything that happened under Operation London Bridge. She worked closely with the Silver Commander, Karen Findlay. Jane Connors has reported that "This was UK policing at its finest". Notice that she didn't say "Met policing at its finest". This is because of the support from various forces throughout the country. It was a unified effort.

Other police officers mentioned in the Met Police short video "Unseen, Operation London Bridge, Policing the funeral of Queen Elizabeth II" include Lisa Hudson and Helen Millichap.

Lisa Hudson was in charge of leading the planning team under the role of Inspector in the Public Order Planning Department for the Met. Helen Millichap, Commander in Specialist Operations had responsibility for royalty, specialists, parliamentary and diplomatic protection. She mentioned in the Met Police clip that Operation London Bridge was also the "biggest traffic plan ever initiated across London to keep people safe."

I can only imagine the accountability these police officers felt in having this responsibility for such a momentous public operation. As I researched the operation, I also found it uplifting to see so many female officers with prominent roles. It seems almost fitting considering the great female monarch we are saying goodbye to.

As I exit security pondering on the operation in hand, I am met by further police. Armed this time, standing like soldiers guarding the whole operation. I hadn't noticed them but of course they would have noticed anything and everything.

Earlier today, one of these armed police officers was my brother. I cannot imagine the concentration needed for such work. I believe they have breaks regularly in order to hold their concentration whilst on shift. Having moved from being an on the street bobby, my brother is now in the armed police and has completed just over 20 years of service.

He followed my Dad's footsteps into the Metropolitan Police. I feel very proud of them both for having a vocation such as this. The aim of which is to make society a better place. They certainly weren't in the police for the money or the holidays or the easy shifts.

I believe my Dad's career started during the 1970's. The only thing I know about 1970's police life is the drama 'Life on Mars'. Whether this is a true reflection of police at the time or not I do not know. I imagine much of it is exaggerated in order to gain viewers. My dad retired after 30 years service in 2002. I remember him receiving his long service medal from the Commissioner and his retirement party at the Metropolitan Police Sports Ground in Chigwell. A place of many a happy childhood afternoons with picnics, bikes, games and ice cream.

His Dad, my Grandad Jack, was also a man of service. Sadly, I was never to meet him as he died suddenly aged just 59 two years before I was born. I feel in some way I have met him though. Through my dad. Everyone says he had a lovely nature and was a kind man. This has been passed on to my dad. You can't joke about people to my dad. Everyone in life and society matters to him.

My Grandad worked as a civil servant and was responsible for leading on computerising a pension system in the 1970's. He was due to receive an OBE on the day that he died. The award was announced in the supplement to The London Gazette on Friday 10th June 1977. He died on 6th June 1977, the Queen's Silver Jubilee. His death was four days before this publication recognising his 31 years of service to the Crown Agents for Overseas Governments and Administrations.

My Grandad had also been a soldier in World War Two. Whilst stationed in Belgium he met a young local woman at a dance. He married her and brought her home to England. She spoke Flemish and French and learnt English. I only wish the languages had carried on through to my generation but like many with English as a second language, the first language is lost within just one generation.

My Grandma was a nurse, again a vocation of service. Thinking about my other grandparents I know my nanny would have loved to have heard all about the queue and the lying in state. We had a connection through our love of Rodgers and Hammerstein films. I love nothing more than a bit of escapism with Carousel, State Fair or the classic The Sound of Music. My nan also enjoyed bingo. Something that all the ladies of my family are a little prone to. My nan worked on a pet market stall in Romford Market. We enjoyed saying hi to her when shopping and getting a bag of treats for our lovely dog Barney. Saturday shopping often ended up back at hers with fish and chips at their family home in North Street. Sadly, she died quite suddenly in 2004.

My maternal Grandad was to be found, on our visits, in his rocking chair. He liked it when my brother had a good haircut and he liked our DM boots saying how sensible they were. I remember him giving us all a £2 coin when they first came out and I felt like it was real treasure.

My Grandad worked at the local brewery. We visited him there sometimes and had a coke. It always felt like such a treat. He always pretended to get our names wrong when we visited and as a child I truly believed he was unsure of who we were but my mum assures me he was just joking. My Grandad died in 1998.

The only one of them that survived to 'old age' was my recently passed Grandma. The only one that got to know me as an adult and that I knew as an adult was Grandma.

I think of all of them as the queue comes to an end. I am reminded of my thoughts earlier. The queue itself is a journey, like a pilgrimage with time to reflect. It has certainly been quite the experience. I am taking so many people in my heart with me to see the Queen lying in state.

Sometimes on a pilgrimage you come to some realisations. I have come to realise that it isn't just a case of me paying respects on behalf of everyone. I feel as though this act I am undertaking is actually me paying respects to all of those people that were once in my life. Paying my respects to the Queen encompasses paying my respects to all those we have loved and lost.

We pass the armed police and suddenly there isn't an orderly queue. Instead, the queue widens and it is ten people wide as we huddle towards the entrance to Westminster Hall. I quickly text Paul,

"About to go in" and switch my phone off. Before we know it we are ushered forwards and climbing some stone steps inside the hall.

We have made it. The time is 1.45am. 12 hours since we first joined the queue all the way back in Southwark Park.

Chapter 16
Westminster Hall

As we walk into Westminster Hall, the largest and oldest hall in Westminster, a quietness takes over everyone and there is silence. Westminster is a world heritage site and I am pleased to report that it is grade one listed. Janet nudges me and whispers,

"Remember to look at the roof, it's really old." I kick myself for having not read about the history of the hall in advance. Never mind, I will take it all in whilst here and then find out afterwards.

The queue of ten people wide continues up the steps. Some people that were behind us get in front and some people that were in front of us get behind. No one minds. British politeness is at its best. Soon we are at the top of the steps and standing below a large stained glass window.

The stained glass window commemorates all those associated with the Palace of Westminster that died in the Second World War. It was designed by Sir Ninian Comper and replaced the previous window that was destroyed by the bombing. Standing below it and looking out at the grand Westminster Hall and to Her Majesty Queen Elizabeth II lying in state is an incredible experience. It is much grander than the TV would have you believe. Wow is the only word that comes to mind. It is the most magnificent space and the most magnificent sight. I would say it is one of those moments in life when you have a numinous feeling and feel as though there is the presence of something greater than you. I am not just Laura in this moment but part of something bigger, greater, historical and spiritual.

The hall has been used for various important occasions. Coronation feasts, courts of law and lying in state are just some of these. The most unusual lying in state to be held was in 1930 when 48 victims of the R101 airship crash lay in state whilst 90,000 people paid their respects. Other more high profile lying in state candidates have included Winston Churchill, Queen Elizabeth the Queen Mother, Edward VII and Queen Mary the widow of George V.

With regards to Queen Elizabeth II, ceremonial addresses were given to her in Westminster Hall in 1977 (Silver Jubilee), 2002 (Golden Jubilee) and 2012 (Diamond Jubilee).

Pope Benedict XVI, Nelson Mandela and Barack Obama have all addressed parliament in Westminster Hall. It holds a significant place in history.

Westminster Hall has also been used as a court of law. Three notable cases include the sentencing of William Wallace, Thomas More and Guy Fawkes. To be in the room where they were condemned to death is eerie and moving. Although we know these are not fictional characters of history, somehow it is only now that I am considering them as real people as I walk in their footsteps.

I suddenly realise that I still have my dog coat on. I have told Paul to look out for my navy jumper with big white writing on, so I need to take the coat off.

I start to take off my coat before descending the steps. I drop it and have to fumble around. I am probably making the most noise at this point and do my best to be as quiet as possible. As I place my bag on the floor and crouch down the man who ran up to the coffin earlier to try and grab it comes to mind. I glance around for evacuation exits and realise that flat on the floor would have to do if some such incident should take place whilst I am in here. Thankfully I am not put in the position of having to be so dramatic.

The queue begins to break up into four smaller queues. With my coat safely in my rucksack, Janet and I edge towards the third queue heading down the steps. The first and fourth queue are 'outer queues' and the second and third are 'inner queues' that are front row in passing the coffin.

The double up of queues each side was a decision taken some days ago to speed up the vast crowds coming to pay their respects. I am pleased. Without this decision my feet may have had to queue for double the time. The queue itself was said to be 10 miles long. 7 miles from Southwark Park to Westminster and 3 miles of snake queueing.

As we descend the steps I remember to look at the roof. In fact, time stands still. The walking down of the stone steps is slow and peaceful. Once again much more so than it seems to be on the TV.

I take a moment to drown in it all. I cannot believe the magnitude of the hall. I know early visitors in the 14th century were wowed by the roof and the lack of pillars creating the vast open space. I am in the 21st century and I too am wowed by it. The roof is an amazing piece of intricate woodwork. Known as 'The Hammerbeam Roof'. It is the largest of its kind in the world. Little work has been done to restore it over the years and just under 10% of the wood has been replaced. You will be glad to know that the replacement wood was taken from oak trees that were fully grown in the 14th century and so could easily have been used for the original. Therefore, 90% of the roof is original and 100% is from 14th century wood.

As is commonplace in the history of London, no historical building is without its share of fires and rebuilding. The hall was remodelled soon after the build in the 14th century by Richard II and much of the stonework seen is from the 19th century. However, Westminster Hall itself and its roof have done a marvellous job in surviving fire and bombs. In 1834 a fire spread throughout Westminster Palace but Westminster Hall was saved.

Charles Barry is a renowned name associated with Westminster. Having won a competition to design the rebuild following the fire, he spent the next 25 years on the project.

In 1941 bombs fell in London and the roof of Westminster Hall caught fire as well as the commons chamber. The commons chamber was sacrificed in order to save the historic Westminster Hall.

As I edge nearer to the Queen's coffin, step by step, I cannot help but feel part of the history of this great hall. Guards of honour add to the ambience by guarding the four corners of the Queen lying in state. The red, yellow and blue Royal Standard flag covers her coffin. Representing the monarchy and the UK this flag should never fly at half mast as there will always be a monarch to reign, even after the death of a King or Queen.

The Sovereign's Orb sits atop the flag. It is in effect a gold ball encrusted with jewels and a cross. It symbolises the monarch's power has been given by God. It was created over 350 years ago in 1661. It is kept in place by being screwed onto the coffin lid.

The Sovereign's sceptre is also on top of the coffin for the lying in state. Also created in 1661 for the coronation of King Charles II it again represents the crown's power. It holds the largest diamond in the world, the 530.2 Cullinan I diamond said to be priceless. No wonder there are so many armed police around.

The Imperial State Crown is the third and final piece sitting on top of the coffin. Created in 1937 to replace previous versions it holds 2,901 precious stones. Most notably it includes the Cullinan II diamond, St Edward's Sapphire, the Stuart Sapphire and the Black Prince's Ruby. St Edward's Sapphire originally belonged to Edward the Confessor back in 1042. It is over 1,000 years old. I am pleased to say I spent time having a good look at all this treasure in front of me. I didn't see it so much as treasure in itself, but a part of the representation of Queen Elizabeth II. Through these items in this great hall we could become closer to her. Despite the numbers, the whole time in the hall felt personal as though no one else was there.

I look down at my own treasure. My sapphire and diamond ring. Always worn to give me good luck.

It has its own history.

It may not be over 1,000 years old but it is over 100 years old. It belonged to my great grandmother Emily Sarah, known in our family as Mem. In particular she holds a very special place in my mum's heart. With my nan having had nine children, my mum became particularly close to her grandmother. She died in 1980, when I was just one year old. I don't remember her but I know that she was kind and loving and family meant everything to her. Just like my mum. I must remember to text mum once I'm out. She will be the one waking in the night checking her phone to see that I am home safe.

She has given her life to looking after us 'children'. Having four children all within six years by the age of 26 is no mean feat, yet she made it look easy. Always there for us when we were unwell with a doughnut and cream soda. She used to push the sofas together and make up a bed for us so we could be downstairs with her all day and watch Pebble Mill and Button Moon. She was at the school gates every day picking us up along with the children that she childminded. She used to make our lunches, iron, cook, play in the sand on holiday. The list goes on. I rarely remember seeing my mum sitting down relaxing. Except of course on those long summer evenings that seemed to be endless in the 1980's.

When my mum gave me Mem's ring it became the most important piece of my jewellery. I tell everyone the story that it is my great grandmother Emily Sarah's ring. It is no wonder that my mum's first child was named Sarah. The second one Emma. You can see the pattern.

In 2012 my second daughter was born and we named her Emily Sarah. I can only hope that she has the kindness and strength of Mem and my mum.

Talking of names my Amy Elizabeth Jane was named after me Laura Jane and my great aunt Bella, Mem's daughter. Her name was Isabella Elizabeth. She was like a nan to us all, living alongside my nanny and grandad with her son being brought up alongside the nine siblings. Always there to babysit with sweets for us all and to give us her honest advice during our teenage years. Along with my grandparents, Mem and Bella will always have a special place in my heart.

I twiddle my ring linking the past to the present as I am taking it all in here in Westminster Hall. It is a solemn affair. As we descend further, I stand to the side a couple of times so that Paul can catch my jumper and pinpoint me on the live stream. Janet is in front of me, with pink coat, again easily recognisable.

As we reach the bottom of the steps, I take time to look at the nearest guard of honour to me. He is looking down and holding his position, but I notice his eyes are moving and I catch his eye briefly. If our minds could talk it would probably go something like this.

"Quite the job you have there this evening."

"You're telling me."

"Busy tonight?"

"Not bad, steady stream."

"Long to go on your shift?"

"Another hour."

"Not long then, enjoy the rest when it comes."

It would be the same polite conversation everyone has with someone who is working when you are not, from the cab drivers to the supermarket cashiers. After our imaginary conversation, I smile and look ahead. It will soon be our turn.

We are pleased to be in the front row for passing the lying in state. Everyone holds back as each person has their moment with the Queen. Janet goes first. She walks up, bows her head and I can see tears in her eyes. It is an extremely moving and privileged moment.

Now it's my turn. I walk to the centre and I bow my head and make the sign of the cross. In my mind I say,

"Thank you for your service from us all". Not that I am more than one, but I have felt throughout the queue an overwhelming responsibility of representing many people. My family, my friends, those who have died. All have been with me on this journey and many would have liked to join me. I look up and hold my gaze for a few seconds and move forwards.

There is still ample space and plenty of room before exiting the hall. The walk away from the coffin to the exit takes as long as the walk towards it. Again, this is something you don't pick up on the live stream. Everyone walks out slowly looking back over their shoulder at the sight before them.

As we finally walk out of the hall, we are met by many armed police once more. We are ushered out of the grounds of Westminster and gather just outside the gates. All the roads are closed, armed police surround and it is a surreal moment standing there in the night air after 12 hours of queueing. We have done it. Everyone that was in the queue with us have rejoined each other and one of the group take a photo. I too begin taking some photos of Westminster.

Big Ben reads six minutes past three. We start talking with a policeman. I take the opportunity to ask where I can get a taxi. He points over Westminster Bridge and tells us to head for St. Thomas' Hospital.

We begin to walk over Westminster Bridge. As we get to the end where we waited for the bag drop, we see the queue. It seems to have come to a standstill. People are sitting and lying on the pavement with foil blankets. Another health and safety risk assessment decision I'm sure. It's early morning and the queuers look cold and tired. Janet has plans to head to Victoria Station with the aunt and nieces. We are all heading that way via St. Thomas' Hospital.

As we are about to cross the road at the end of Westminster Bridge where traffic is allowed, I spot a very welcome sight. Very handily a black taxi pulls up at the traffic lights with its light on. Quick as a flash I stick my arm out and he undoes the window.

"Can you take me to Chingford?" I say hopefully.

"Jump in" comes the reply. Wow that was easier than expected. I quickly say goodbye to Janet and co and jump into the taxi.

I settle comfortably into the back of the taxi and before I can stop myself the words are out and I hear myself saying, "Busy tonight?"

Epilogue

The first thing I did in the taxi was text my mum.

"In taxi on way home". It was almost 3.30am. I knew she would be relieved to know that I was not wandering the streets of London anymore. I was home by 4.15am. Once home and in bed I began to shiver. All that time outside queueing and yet it was when I was all snug under the covers that my body decided to be cold. It took me an hour to fall asleep.

The next morning as I swung my legs out of bed I could hardly move. My feet! They were suffering but I wasn't. I felt elated at my experience. I got myself down to the front room to watch the live stream. Paul told me that he had seen me so I was looking forward to it.

With my customary cup of tea I began to watch. There I was! Navy jumper with white writing coming down the stairs behind Janet. Wow, what a memory captured visually. As we descended the stairs the camera caught the solemnity of the experience. What it didn't capture was the vastness of Westminster Hall.

The camera stayed on Janet who was now at the front of the queue. She stepped forward and bowed her head. My turn next. I was looking forward to seeing my big moment. I watch as I walk towards the coffin and... the camera cuts and pans to the other side of the room. Typical. Never mind at least I can relive the walking down the stairs moment time and again.

The rest of the day is spent scanning the crowds for David Q and others so that I can send them screenshots to them. I am successful. They are grateful.

I study the map of the queue to relive what I have walked and something captures my eye. The bag drop is a detour loop. There was no need to walk ten minutes there and ten minutes back and rejoin the queue. We could have all gone together and rejoined the queue much further up had we followed the loop!

With the queue experience behind me, focus turns to preparing for the Queen's funeral. I start the day before by making some coffee and walnut cake, an iced traybake and some shortbread. I'm up and out early in the morning of the day of the funeral to buy the papers, make the sandwiches and cook the sausage rolls. My coffee table is laid with my teapot. I will spend at least the next eight hours saying goodbye to the only monarch that has reigned during my lifetime. It is a momentous occasion. I share texts with Janet David Q. We are bound together in a way only those in the queue understand.

This communication between us continues for future royal events. Charles III first Christmas speech and King Charles and Queen Camilla's Coronation.

The Coronation is a great excuse to buy a new teapot so I treat myself and prepare accordingly. Cake making, paper buying, sausage roll cooking and teapot filling keep me busy. Flags adorn the living room. We look forward. We have now left behind the Elizabethan period and are firmly in the Carolean era. Long live the King!

Bibliography

Arnold, C. (2015) Globe, Life in Shakespeare's London. London: Simon and Schuster UK Ltd.

Bowse, G. (2012) A History of London's Prisons. South Yorkshire: Wharncliffe Books.

Brandon, D. & Brooke, A. (2013) Bankside, London's Original District of Sin. Gloucestershire: Amberley Publishing.

Burford, E. J. (1989) A short history of The Clink Prison. London: E.J. Burford

Favilli, E. & Cavello, F. (2016) Goodnight Stories for Rebel Girls. California: Rebel Girls

Favilli, E. & Cavello, F. (2016) Goodnight Stories for Rebel Girls 2. California: Rebel Girls

Gerhold, D. (2021) London Bridge and It's Houses c. 1209-1761. Oxford: OXBOW books.

Morgan, S. (2022) Queen Elizabeth II. London: Scholastic.

Trustees of the Imperial War Museum (2013) HMS Belfast: Guidebook. London: IWM.

UK Parliament. (2022) The Palace of Westminster, Official Guide. London: UK Parliament.

UK Parliament. (2022) Big Ben and the Elizabeth Tower, Official Guide. London: UK Parliament.

https://www.royalparks.org.uk/parks/victoria-tower-gardens/map-of-victoria-tower-gardens

https://www.guysandstthomas.nhs.uk/about-us/our-history

www.thehistorypress.co.uk/articles/the-reign-of-queen-elizabeth-ii-a-timeline/

https://cathedral.southwark.anglican.org/

https://www.nationalcovidmemorialwall.org/

https://thefreelancehistorywriter.com/2017/04/14/catherine-of-aragons-speech-at-blackfriars-june-1529/

Printed in Great Britain
by Amazon